ISBN 1434826392
www.TeachingArchery.com

Warning:
Archery, like any sport, can be dangerous. No safety equipment, program, or book can replace common sense. Although I've made every effort to present a safe archery instruction system, the final responsibility for safety lies with the archer and instructor. Always be alert when practicing archery, and make safety your first priority.

"What?! I'm teaching archery?"

WHO SHOULD READ THIS BOOK

Though archery instructors range from grandparents teaching grandchildren to professional coaches preparing teens for the Olympics, most archery instructors are average, everyday people who just like to work with kids. They are enlisted by camp directors and volunteer coordinators to work in summer camps and youth programs on a part-time or volunteer basis. And, more often than not, they know little or nothing about bows and arrows.

This book is written for anyone who wants to teach kids about archery. You don't need to be an expert archer yourself to be a safe, effective instructor for young aspiring archers. All you need is a desire to teach archery. In fact, you will probably find that by instructing others, you will be learning a lot yourself, and the kids will challenge you to learn and grow with them.

ARCHERY STUDENTS

Many of the scenarios in this book are designed for a summer camp or similar environment, but with some creativity and enthusiasm they can be adapted to most situations. School physical education programs, youth sports organizations, or even interested parents could find this information equally useful.

Archery is a fun sport that is accessible to a wide range of people, and young archers

QUICK START

If you are a new archery instructor with little experience, don't fear! You can teach archery to kids, and do a darn good job of it. It's likely you got this job because of your enthusiasm, resourcefulness, responsibility, common sense, kid empathy, or all of the above. If you have these traits, then the only other thing you need before you're a first rate archery instructor is information, and this book is full of it. If you're short on time (the kids arrive in a week, let's say) then you should probably read the following sections first, in this order:

➡ Equipment, p. 6, 22, 24, 26
➡ The Range
➡ Preparation
➡ Teaching

come in all types. They are girls and boys, wealthy and poor, able-bodied and disabled. In general, it's difficult to teach kids younger than eight, but in some cases you will find very capable students that are younger... and painfully inattentive ones that are much older.

HOW TO USE THIS BOOK

This book has two tasks. The first is to allow a new instructor with little or no archery experience to quickly get up to speed with the basic knowledge required. If you are new to archery instruction, you'll find the Quick Start on the previous page very helpful. Once you have time, you can go back and read other sections. Save Lore for last; it's a lot of interesting background information on archery, but isn't critical for teaching. It's more useful for answering questions, telling stories, or planning archery programs.

The second task is to serve as a reference book that you can come back to once you've got the basic teaching tasks under control. If you have time, by all means read the whole book. It's intended to serve as a reference for furthering your knowledge of archery and to help you answer questions. People have been writing about archery for almost 500 years (you can read about Roger Ascham in the Lore section), so a lot of information is available. In *Teaching Archery to Kids*, you will find a lot of pertinent facts condensed down and collected in one convenient place. If your question is beyond the scope of this book, then there is a reference section in the back that lists other more exhaustive sources to turn to.

And finally, remember this book is just a guide. Feel free to improvise or ignore it as you see fit; working with kids is full of surprises and requires a great deal of flexibility. Nothing can replace common sense, creativity, and good judgment. The idea is that with this book, you will have a basic guideline to get you started, and a place to return to when you need to know more. It's part cheat-sheet, part fact-book.

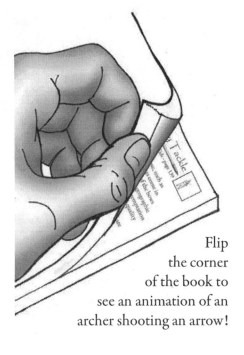

Flip the corner of the book to see an animation of an archer shooting an arrow!

Table of Contents

May the time never come
when
the bend of the Bow
and
the thud of the Arrow
will cease to charm
and send a thrill to the heart
of the Bowman.

-Adolph Shane

Equipment: The Arrow

For good shooting, everything depends upon the arrow. No matter how true your aim, how staunch your bow, or how steady your hand, you cannot hit regularly without perfect arrows.
  -Maurice Thompson, 1878

If you have a poor bow but good arrows, you can still shoot well. But it doesn't work the other way around; no matter how good the bow, poor arrows will always give you poor shots.
  -old archery adage

ABOUT ARROWS

Arrows were once referred to as "cloth-yard shafts", because in the ancient marketplace, a yard of cloth was measured by pulling it edgewise from your left hand to your right ear, much like drawing an arrow. Modern arrows aren't usually a yard long; changes in draw styles and bow weights have made the arrow shorter, around 30 inches or so, depending on the archer and bow.

Arrows must be springy, for two reasons: so as to not shatter when hitting the target, and to allow them to warp around the bow when released (see *archer's paradox* in the Lore section). This springiness is measured by a number called *spine weight*. The spine weight of an arrow is a rough indication of what bow weight it should be shot from for best performance. The higher the number, the stiffer the arrow; for example, a 45-pound spine weight arrow will shoot best from a 45 pound bow. It could be shot from a heavier bow, but it will bend too much during the release, and usually end up right of the target (for a right-handed archer). Likewise, the same arrow shot from a 25-pound bow would be too stiff and land left of target. For more on bow weight, flip to the Equipment: The Bow.

The arrow's mass is an important variable as well. Lighter arrows travel faster and drop less before they hit the target. The tradeoff is that they are more affected by wind, especially at longer ranges. When bowhunting, arrow mass is important because a lighter, faster arrow gives an animal less time to react and sprint away, but a heavier arrow penetrates better and will deflect less if it hits a twig or leaf on the way.

Much like the human body, the arrow has many parts with specific, technical names. Learning an arrow's anatomy will help you to better discuss archery.

Parts of the Arrow

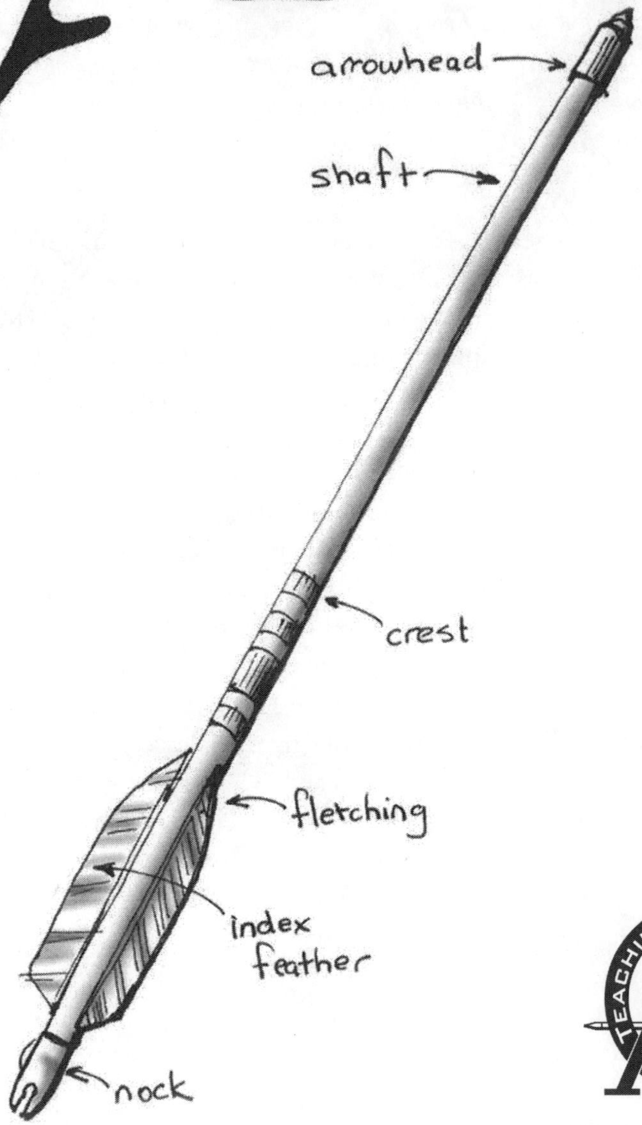

arrowhead →

shaft →

← crest

← fletching

index feather

nock ↙

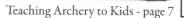

Equipment: The Arrow

ARROWHEAD

The arrowhead is also called a *point* or *pyle*. In more primitive days, they were held to the shaft with a *tang*. This is an extended tab at the back of the arrowhead that slides into a slot in the shaft, and is tied in place. Today, most arrowheads are of the *ferrule* type, where a tube is attached to or hollowed out of the back of the arrowhead, and the shaft is inserted into the tube and held with ferrule cement. It may be interesting to note that the most advanced arrowheads

tang construction

are returning to the ancient tang technique, but with a twist: they have threads on the tang that screw into an insert in the front of the shaft, allowing for a quick-change in the field.

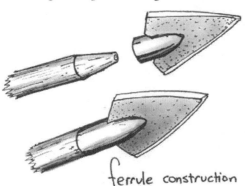

ferrule construction

There are several types of arrowheads listed in the following pages, some with many subtle variations. Since the main purpose of the arrowhead is to focus the energy of the arrow to a point and to ease penetration of the target, arrowhead design generally varies as approriate to the target. Manufactured arrowheads come in standard weight increments, such as 100 grain[1], 125 grain, 150 grain, etc. This allows you to get similar flight characteristics from different types of arrowheads by matching the weight. The following pages show some examples of different arrowheads you might encounter.

---

1. A "grain" is a medieval measure, based on the weight of a grain of wheat. You still see it occasionally in reference to medicine, precious metals, and projectiles. There are 437.5 grains in one ounce.

target point: Made from thin stamped metal, this arrowhead is typical on institutional-grade arrows, and is intended only to be shot into target butts.

field point: Cast from steel, it is heavier and more durable than the target point. This multi-use point has better penetration and can also be used for field archery, stump shooting, and small game hunting.

blunts (several types): Typically used for stump shooting or tricks like shooting cans, they can be made from steel or rubber. Their "safe" look can be deceiving, especially to younger archers. They are quite capable of putting out an eye or tooth, so care must still be used.

improvised point: Resourceful archers put all sorts of things at the business end of their arrows. This example is a .38 handgun shell used as a practice blunt[2].

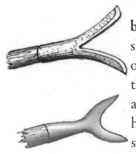

Judo™ point: A proprietary, modified blunt designed for small game hunting. Spring arms prevent the arrow from passing all the way through critters and getting lost in the underbrush beyond. What they're REALLY handy for is stump shooting, though. The spring arms catch in grass and pine needles, so rather than sliding under the grass and being lost, arrows tend to pop upright and are easier to find.

bird points: These are ancient arrowheads intended to shoot birds in flight. The "V" or crescent[3] catches part of the bird, such as a wing or neck, and pulls it in to the center where it can be cut, rather than deflecting it away. There is scholarly uncertainty here, as well: some historical accounts refer to this as a rope-cutter, for slicing rigging during naval battles.

---

2. Howard Hill used these for rabbit hunting.
3. Ascham mentions heads shaped "like the new moon" used for shooting at the necks of birds. He doesn't seem concerned that arrows rotate in flight, making this a chancy proposition at best.

karimata: Literally translated as "hunting fork", this Japanese point was used for both hunting and war[4]. Occasionally a *karimata* and *kaburaya* appear on the same arrow (see *whistling arrowhead*).

Snaro™ point: This is another proprietary design, composed of a blunt head with loops of rigid wire attached, spread out to ensnare a bird in flight. They are available in several sizes.

chisel point: No longer in use, this ancient design was for hunting larger animals. The large, sharp edge causes extensive bleeding.

cornstalk point: A field point with a long, thin steel spike at the end for traditional Cherokee cornstalk shoots (see the section on Activities).

bodkin: A medieval design intended for war. The sharp point helps it penetrate armor, but the pyramid shape makes it strong enough to not crumple as a broadhead might. Often, they were waxed before the battle to aid in penetration.

broadhead: The primary head for hunting larger game, broadheads have a sharp point and thin, razor-sharp edges to cause extensive bleeding in animals. Ancient broadheads were chipped from stone, whereas modern ones are usually high-carbon steel. They break or dull quickly if shot into target butts (not to mention damaging the butt), and are generally dangerous for young archers to even handle due to their extreme sharpness.

broadhead, 3 blade: A variation on the broadhead, designed to cause yet more bleeding. One disadvantage over the flat broadhead is that it might get hung up on the ribcage instead of penetrating vital organs.

---

4.   Thanks to Ukiko Maxwell for translations and research.

broadhead, barbed: A broadhead with rearward-facing points, to prevent arrow removal and increase bleeding. They were used in ancient times for both hunting and warfare. Today, they are banned in most states.

broadhead, mechanical: Invented in the 1980s, this broadhead has a mechanical system that causes the razor edges to swing out upon impact. Theoretically, this allows for truer flight and reduced deflection by branches. Conventional wisdom indicates that this slight advantage is not worth the added complexity and chance for malfunction.

fishing barb: Much like a field point, but with a retractable barb. The barb is necessary when bow fishing, as the arrow's job is to connect the fishing line to the fish, not to kill it (because it would then be pretty hard to retrieve from the water). The arrow pierces the fish, then holds fast as the archer reels in his catch.

flaming arrowhead: These are generally homemade, using a modified field point or broadhead. The shaft is longer also, to protect the archer's bowhand from being scorched while drawing and aiming. These are NOT for use by kids!

whistling arrowhead: Historical texts from China and the East mention these. Crafted skillfully from metal or wood, they were used for signalling or psychological warfare. The Japanese whistling arrowhead is called a *kaburaya*, which translates loosely to "turnip-arrow," in reference to its turnip-like shape. In a ceremony called *yabusame*, archers shoot *kaburaya* at targets while riding a galloping horse.

In addition to the metal arrowheads shown above, arrowheads can be made of other materials such as rubber and glass. Primitive people used bone, stone, shells, animal quills, or the spines of exotic fish. In a pinch, fire hardened wood will even serve.

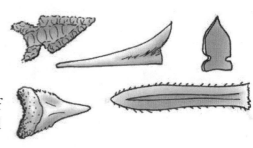

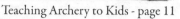

SHAFT

The shaft (or *stele* in ancient books) is the long skinny part of the arrow that makes up most of its essence. The shaft itself is generally a cylinder of uniform diameter, ranging from 1/4" to 23/64" across. Historical and specialty arrows can be 3/8" diameter or larger. Some quality wooden arrows are *barreled*, or get wider towards the midsection of the arrow. This is to make the arrow strongest where the tendency to bend is greatest, while saving weight at the ends. Another uncommon practice is for a shaft to be *chested*, or tapered towards the point. If a shaft tapers towards the fletchings, it's said to be *bobtailed*[5]; the idea is that the stronger front end will be less likely to break when pulled from the target butt.

There are a few broad groups of shaft materials, and each has its benefits and drawbacks:

Wood

This is a broad category. Most institutional grade arrows are wood, usually of pine or some similar softwood. They are light, inexpensive, and durable. If bent, they can be straightened without much fuss. They usually are spined for 25 pound bows, and will have various minor defects when new.

There are also higher quality wood arrows available, made from woods such as Port Orford cedar, Douglas fir, and northern hemlock. These arrows are available in a several standard diameters (1/4", 5/16", 11/32", and 23/64") and spine weights grouped in five-pound clusters. They are generally custom-built by the archer, perform exceedingly well, and are beautiful to behold.

Other plant products are occasionally used for arrow shafts, as well. Native Americans used reeds, and bamboo was popular in parts of Asia. If an arrow is made with a second, harder wood towards the point, it is said to be *footed*.

> *Somehow, I feel that arrows of wood are more in keeping with the real spirit of old-time archery and require more of the archer himself than a more modern arrow; maybe that is a silly reason for shooting wooden arrows, but most of us archers are silly, one way or another. Call it sentiment if you like.*
> *-Howard Hill, 1953*

---

5.   Shane (1936) p.66

Metal

The market on aluminum arrows is largely cornered by Easton, Inc and has been since they first made aluminum arrows in 1939. Aluminum arrows are relatively expensive and easily damaged, but are perfectly uniform and provide flawless precision. Charts from the manufacturer will help you select the perfect combination of weight, stiffness, and diameter to match your bow. Often viewed as the only choice for competitive shooting, they aren't as good for beginners because they can bend and break when they aren't shot into an appropriate target butt. They are multi-purpose as well; oftentimes they have interchangeable screw-in heads, allowing the same arrow to be used for target shooting, stump shooting, and bowhunting.

Fiberglass

Fiberglass arrows are uncommon except for one specialty use: bowfishing. Unlike wood, they don't swell and warp when wet, and unlike aluminum, they can take terrible abuse without being ruined. Their downfall is that they are relatively heavy and unwieldy.

Carbon fiber/ graphite

This is a relatively modern material. It produces a stiff, light, uniform arrow that outperforms even aluminum. However, it is even less forgiving of any abuse. To make matters worse, a carbon fiber arrow that is damaged may not appear so until shot, at which point it could literally explode, sending pieces into the archer or bystanders. This high-performance arrow is not recommended for inexperienced archers.

CREST

The crest is the striped pattern that is painted on the arrow just in front of the fletching. It is not required, but this ancient tradition serves a practical purpose. Each archer has their own pattern of colors and stripe widths that can be used to identify their arrows. It's handy when several people are shooting at the same target, when arrows miss and go into the woods, or even when you go back to the lost and found arrow barrel at the range a week after the last time you shot. Young archers with their own equipment should be encouraged to invent their own crest and put it on their arrows. In an institutional setting, it is good to for the instructor to group arrows with similar crests together in the same quivers, to aid in scoring.

Equipment: The Arrow

EQUIPMENT

FLETCHING

The fletching (or *shaftment* in ancient books) is the group of feathers at the back end of the arrow. Its main job is to aerodynamically stabilize the arrow and prevent it from tumbling in flight. The fletching can be made in several different combinations of size, profile, and arrangement.

Most fletchings are four to six inches long, depending on the application, but other sizes are available. Smaller fletchings increase arrow speed because they produce less drag, and larger fletchings are needed to balance heavier points such as broadheads or Judo points.

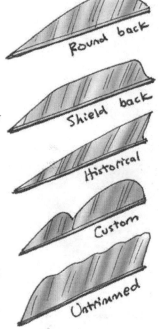

Typical profiles include round-back, shield-back, parabolic, and untrimmed. Historical and custom shaped feathers can be made as well. In general, the actual shapes of the feathers have only a slight impact on flight characteristics if their overall sizes are similar.

The fletchings are arranged on the shaft in a slight spiral. This *helical fletching* causes the arrow to spin in flight, gyroscopically stabilizing it and also averaging out any microscopic imbalances that might be in the arrow, so it can fly straight and true (see the section on arrow construction & repair in Crafts for more on this). There are a few basic fletching arrangements:

three-feather fletching: This is by far the most common arrangement, with three feathers spaced equally around the shaft in 120° increments. One feather is set perpendicular to the bowstring, and that is referred to as the *index feather*. The index feather faces away from the bow, so that when shot, the other two feathers glance past the bow and disrupt flight as little as possible. A colorful bit if trivia: the index feather is sometimes called the *cock feather*, and the other two are the *hen feathers*... though this has nothing to do with which type of fowl they come from.

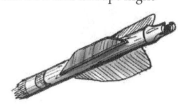

four-feather fletching: Four feathers, each angled 30° off of the bowstring. It's not clear where this came from historically, but it has both advantages and disadvantages over three-feather fletching. The disadvantage is that it weighs 33% more, slowing arrow flight slightly. The advantage is that with this design, there is no index feather to look for; either way you nock it, no feather will hit the limb of the bow dead-on. Fletchings for this arrangement can be a little smaller than for an equivalent three-feather design.

six-feather fletching (flu-flu): The flu-flu fletching is designed to cause a lot of drag, acting like a parachute for your arrow. Flu-flu arrows are meant to be shot at things above you, like birds or squirrels or toss-targets, so the arrow will slow rapidly after it misses a target, and fall harmlessly back down to earth in the same general area as the archer. Feathers for flu-flus are generally left large and untrimmed.

spiral flu-flu fletching: This is another variation of the flu-flu, in this case the feather is wound around the shaft in a tight spiral, and all the individual fibers of the feather are ruffled out to catch as much wind as possible.

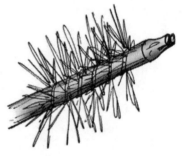

Materials

A few different materials are used for fletching, with various advantages and disadvantages:

➤ Feathers: The original fletching material, feathers have a certain magic because they come from flying creatures, and are familiar with the ways of the wind. Birds and arrows value the same traits: light weight, high strength, aerodynamic smoothness, and great rigidity. Feathers from any large bird will do, but turkey and goose are the most commonly available. They look good in their natural state, or can be dyed bright colors. They are trimmed to various shapes that have debatable difference in effectiveness. It is worth noting that all the feathers on an arrow should be from the same wing of the bird, either right wing or left wing, so they all curve the same direction.

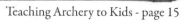

➺ Vanes: Feather-shaped pieces of vinyl or plastic. They have the advantage of being a little more durable and resistant to water, but their downside is that they are often too stiff in cold weather. In some ancient cultures, vanes of leather or even thin pieces of wood were used in place of feathers.

➺ Parchment: Thin pieces of paperlike parchment were used by ancient Turks, to make their arrows lighter and able to travel farther. These fletchings were usually very small, only 2 ½" long and ¼" high.

➺ Molded plastic: Occasionally on REALLY cheap arrows, you will see the fletching and nock all molded together from plastic, connected to a slip-on tube that covers the back few inches of the shaft. It works for getting the arrow downrange, but even novice archers will soon want to abandon this and move up to real fletchings.

NOCK

The *nock* is a small cut or notch in the back of the arrow, designed to fit onto the bowstring. Ancient arrows had *self-nocks*, where the shaft itself was notched to accept the bowstring, then wound with several wraps of cord or reinforced with horn to prevent the shaft from splitting when shot. Today, plastic nocks are the norm. These molded clips have a tapered ferrule designed to be glued to the back end of the shaft. They come in bright colors, to make it easier to find your arrows in the underbrush. Some have little fins or bumps on one side, to allow the archer to quickly identify the index feather side of the arrow by feel.

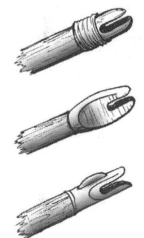

Equipment: The Bow

The bow... stands for all that is clever and fine in woodcraft...
-Handbook for Boys, Boys Scouts of America (1911 edition)

ABOUT BOWS

Though there are many different designs and materials for bows, there are a few combinations that are tried and true. A typical institutional bow at a summer camp or school will likely be made from fiberglass, with a recurve design. Occasionally, better equipped programs will have recurve bows available that are of wood and fiberglass composite construction. Compound bows are popular with the bowhunting crowd, and will sometimes appear at classes where students bring their own bows. Historical societies, reenactors, and traditionalists will be seen shooting longbows and flatbows.

Even if your program only has one kind of bow, it's good to be familiar with the types and materials of bows so you can answer questions from the more inquisitive students.

Most bows will be marked with maker's information, usually on the belly or near the handle. A cryptic message such as the one shown to the right tells you everything you need to know about the bow. The first line indicates the proper string size: 54 inches long, AMO[1]. The second line tells you that the bow will take 24 pounds of pull to draw it to its designed draw length of 28 inches. Drawing it past that length will give unpredictable results, and could damage or destroy the bow. Drawing it less than the draw length will not yield the full weight, and will cause your arrows to be underpowered.

When selecting a bow, a 28-inch draw length is adequate for all except very short or very tall archers. Generally, a bow's draw weight should be as much as you can comfortably pull. All else being equal, higher weights mean faster arrow speed. Faster arrows have more penetrating power, drop off less at longer ranges, and are less affected by the wind. However, all the speed in

---

1. Generally, AMO (Archery Manufacturing Organization) length is 4 inches longer than actual length.

the world will do you no good if you can't hold the bow at full draw long enough for a careful, steady aim.

BOW SHAPES

Bow come in many shapes; here are some general categories that will help to sort them out. Some bows will fall into more than one category, or have characteristics of several.

Recurve

This simple, efficient design is quite common in institutional settings like summer camps and schools, because it is so simple yet effective. A recurve bow has tips that bend towards the back of the bow (towards the target, when you're holding it). This curvature gives the bow a little more power right as the arrow leaves the string, making the arrow travel faster and straighter. Larger, heavier recurve bows will usually have a riser section and some *deflex*, or bend in the handle away from the target.

Longbow

Longbows are made from straight pieces of wood, and when unstrung can be as tall as the archer. Often, their limbs are "D" shaped in cross section, and are nearly as thick as they are wide. They are an ancient and romantic design, able to develop much more draw weight than shorter bows, but are not as efficient as recurve designs and are much harder to pull near full draw.

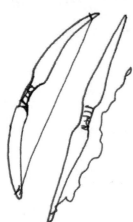

Flatbow

Flatbows are short, straight bows with limbs that are several times wider than they are thick. This type of bow is a traditional style that puts lower stresses on the limbs, making it a durable and forgiving design. It was used by many ancient peoples, including most of the Native American tribes; a notable exception to this are the Cherokee, who used longbows very similar to those of the medieval English.

Compound

A modern design, compound bows are the product of careful engineering and manufacture. They use multiple strings and eccentric cams (wheels) at the tips to create a mechanical advantage at full draw, much like using a pulley or lever. This has a twofold purpose: it makes the bowstring's tension the greatest right as the arrow leaves the string (when it's needed the most), and it aids in careful aiming by reducing the felt draw weight at full draw. This *letoff* might result in a bow that shoots an arrow with 70 pounds of force, yet takes only 40 pounds to hold at full draw.

BOW MATERIALS

A bow can be made out of almost anything flexible, but these materials are the most common:

Fiberglass

A modern, man-made material, fiberglass comes in many different colors, or is transparent. It is easily identifiable by its "plastic" look, and is very common on lower-end bows that you might see at institutions such as schools and summer camps. It has many advantages: it is durable, waterproof, heat resistant, and inexpensive. Besides its relative ugliness, its only minor drawback is that it doesn't perform quite as well as some other materials.

Metal

Aluminum, steel, and magnesium are commonly used in compound bows. These bows require the amazing strength and springiness of metal to drive the cams and strings that launch arrows at compound-bow speed. Occasionally you will see a recurve bow made entirely of metal, but this practice was only common for a few years in the sixties.

Wood

The original bow material, wood is still the most beautiful thing to make a bow out of. It comes from the good earth, and embodies the true spirit of archery. This material is generally not good for beginners, though, as wood bows are easily broken, dented , or twisted. When they break, they break catastrophically, sending pieces everywhere (including into bystanders). Wood bows also require regular care and maintenance.

Composite

Some bows are a mix of several materials. A common example is a wood bow with fiberglass laminations on the back and belly.

This can give you the best of both worlds: the high performance and beauty of wood, with the durability and strength of fiberglass. Lightweight metals like aluminum are sometimes used in risers and handles to save weight. Ancient Eastern bowyers combined horn and sinew to make very effective composite bows that could shoot arrows over 200 yards.

BOW PARTS

Here's a quick breakdown on the parts of the bow. Not all bows will have all of the parts listed, but you can generally expect to find the following parts on these types of bows:

Recurve Bow	Compound Bow	Camp Bow
limbs	limbs	limbs
belly & back	belly & back	belly & back
handle	handle	handle
riser	riser	
rest or shelf	rest	shelf
sight	sight	
bowstring	bowstring	bowstring
nocking point	nocking point	nocking point
serving	serving	serving
	silencers	
	kisser	
	peep	
	cables (top & bottom)	
	cable guard	
	tear drop	
stabilizer ferrule	stabilizer ferrule	
string nock		string nock
	cams & eccentric pulleys	

back & belly: The back of the bow is the part that faces away from you as you hold the bow in the shooting position, pointing towards the target. The belly is the side that faces towards you. When you draw a bow, the back goes into tension (stretches) and the belly goes into compression (squashes).

cable: On a compound bow, the cables are the strings that do not touch the arrow. They are usually made of woven steel cable due to the immense stress they must withstand.

cable guard: The cable guard only appears on compound bows; it is a little rod that points back towards the archer and keeps the cables from contacting the arrow.

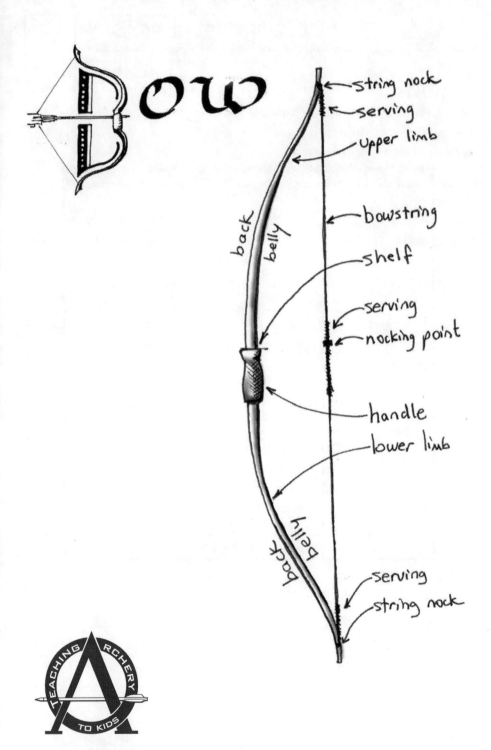

Bow

string nock
serving
upper limb
bowstring
shelf
serving
nocking point
handle
lower limb
serving
string nock

back
belly

belly
back

TEACHING ARCHERY TO KIDS

Equipment: The Bow

EQUIPMENT

cam: This lopsided wheel is the magic part that makes a compound bow work. As the archer draws a compound bow, the cams rotate at the end of the limbs, and the effective length of the bow changes. This increases the mechanical advantage and reduces the draw weight.

eccentric pulley: Though very similar to a cam and serving exactly the same purpose, an eccentric pulley is not actually lopsided; it just has the axle mounted off-center (eccentrically). One is often mistaken for the other.

kisser button: A small plastic disk woven into the bowstring to ensure a proper anchor point. When the button touches the corner of your mouth, you are at full draw.

limb: The limbs are the curved, flexible part of the bow; the spring that stores the energy of the draw.

nocking point: This is a knot of floss or a metal clip that is permanently affixed to the bowstring to mark the correct, consistent location for nocking the arrow onto the string.

peep sight: Similar to a kisser button, this is a little tube woven into the bowstring just above the serving. You look through it and across a sight at the front of the bow, ensuring proper alignment.

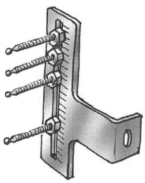

pin sight: The pin sight attaches to the riser of your bow, and consists of a metal bar with adjustable pins bolted through it. The pins represent different ranges, and can be adjusted in and out as well as up and down for each individual archer. When the tip of the pin is put over the bull at full draw, a clean release will ensure a perfect hit. Some have colored balls, lights, or other variations at the tips of the pins.

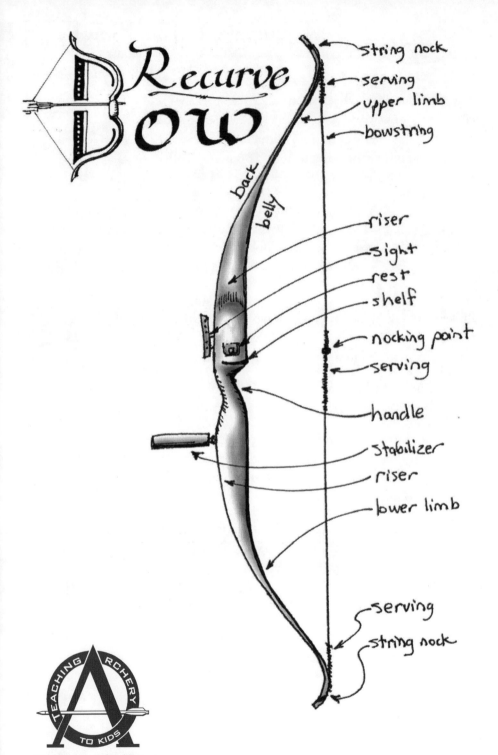

Recurve Bow

- string nock
- serving
- upper limb
- bowstring

back
belly

- riser
- sight
- rest
- shelf
- nocking point
- serving
- handle
- stabilizer
- riser
- lower limb
- serving
- string nock

TEACHING ARCHERY TO KIDS

rest: There are a few different types of rests, but the most basic is simply a piece of smooth leather glued to the top of the shelf to reduce friction. A slightly more sophisticated version is the "rug rest", a piece of fuzz that does the same thing, but reduces friction further by lifting the arrow onto tiny fibers. Some bows with shoot-through risers have a "flipper rest", a tiny plastic or metal arm that cradles the arrow during the draw.

riser: The riser is the massive, unbending center part of the bow. It is quite large on some bows, and nonexistent on others. Generally, the larger the riser, the more stable the bow will be. Many modern bows have "shoot-through" risers, where much of the riser is cut away near the rest, allowing the arrow to travel straight along the path of travel of the string, reducing or eliminating archer's paradox (see p. 164).

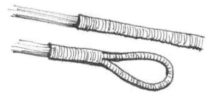

serving: To protect against wear on the bowstring, this second abrasion-resistant string is wrapped around the bowstring at high-wear locations such as the loops and the center.

shelf: The shelf is the flat part on top of the handle where the arrow sits during the draw. On some bows, there is a shelf on both sides of the handle, allowing for right- or left-handed use. On other bows, like many longbows, there is no shelf at all.

silencer: Bowstring silencers consist of plastic whiskers or a piece of fur that is woven through the strands of the bowstring towards each end. They soak up some of the "twang" from the bowstring, quieting the shot.

stabilizer: These come in many sizes and configurations. They mount to the bow, and stick out as rods or wands to the front or sides. Their job is to dampen vibrations and sway.

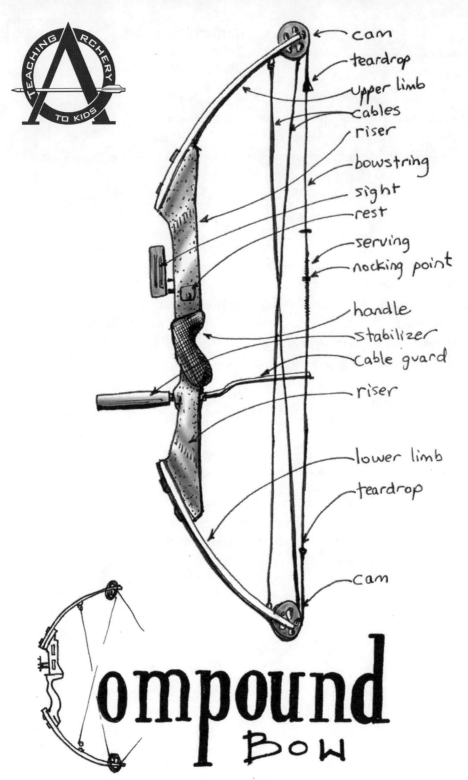

cam
teardrop
upper limb
cables
riser
bowstring
sight
rest
serving
nocking point
handle
stabilizer
cable guard
riser
lower limb
teardrop
cam

Compound Bow

© 2008, Jim "Fletch" Fanjoy

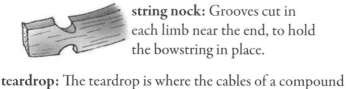

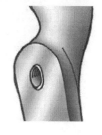

stabilizer ferrule: This is a hole in the front of the riser or handle of the bow, with a threaded steel insert. It allows stabilizers, bowfishing reels, or other accessories to be screwed into the bow.

string nock: Grooves cut in each limb near the end, to hold the bowstring in place.

teardrop: The teardrop is where the cables of a compound bow connect to the bowstring; they are sometimes double-sided to facilitate changing out bowstrings without a bow press. There are no string nocks on a compound bow.

BOWSTRINGS

Bowstring is actually made from multiple strands of string, of varying materials. Though ancient bowstrings were made from sinew, hide, flax, or other fibers, most bowstrings today will be made from one of the following materials:

➤ Dacron B50: The most popular bowstring material. Affordable, stronger than linen, manmade, more durable. Usually black, but available in other colors as well.

➤ Fast-Flite: Another man-made material, Fast-Flite is stronger and less elastic than B50. It is considered the ultimate bowstring material. It imparts a lot of shock to the bow, though, and shouldn't be used on older bows or bows that aren't specifically designed for it.

➤ Nylon: A manmade material with a lot of stretch, it makes a pretty poor bowstring. About the only thing going for it is how inexpensive it is; that might be why you see it occasionally on cheap bows. It is usually white, unlike the other manmade materials.

➤ Linen: It is a strong natural material, but degrades quickly in damp environments. Unless dyed, it is off-white or taupe in color.

➤ Silk: This natural fiber was used by ancient archers in Asia, but is extremely rare in the western hemisphere in the modern era.

➤ Sinew: Made from tendons of animals, sinew is not a fantastic bowstring material because it stretches (very badly if wet), but it was all that was available to many primitive cultures. You're not likely to see it in a teaching environment.

There are two numbers that are used to describe a bowstring when ordering or making one, much like on the bow itself. Draw weight is the weight of bow it was designed for, in pounds. A string that is too light for a bow might break when shot, and a string that is overly heavy for a bow is safe but will rob the arrow of speed. AMO length is a standardized length set by the Archery Manufacturing Organization. It is measured differently for different kinds of bows, but is generally equal to the actual length of the string plus four inches. Again, a string that is too long or too short will adversely affect performance, and may damage the bow. It is best to always use a string that matches the specifications on the bow's label. There are several bowstring designs available; here are some of the most common:

Continuous loop: This bowstring looks like it is made from twelve to sixteen straight strands with a loop at each end. In actuality, it is made from one really long piece of string, wound round and round from string nock to string nock to give the effect of multiple straight strands. It has reinforcing (called *serving*) wrapped around the ends and middle. These strings allow the least stretch and are the best for general use in a teaching environment.

Flemish: These strings are twisted and tied in a traditional way that dates back to the middle ages, and are better described in the Crafts section. One end of the string is left without a loop, and is tied onto the string nock with a timber hitch to allow you to adjust the *fistmele* of your bow (more on that at the end of the Preparation section). Flemish strings are mostly for traditionalists or historical reenactors.

Woven: Woven bowstrings look like they are braided, and this design allows for far more stretch than is desirable. Nylon bowstrings are typically woven, combining the worst design with the worst material. Luckily, woven bowstrings usually only appear on really cheap bows.

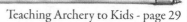

There is no archer in the world who can consistently shoot better than his equipment.
-Howard Hill, 1953

TACKLE: IT'S ALL ABOUT THE ACCESSORIES

A bow and an arrow are *technically* all you need for archery, but there are a few other pieces of tackle that can make shooting more enjoyable. Some of the items shown here will see little use while teaching kids to be archers, but are described here to round out the knowledge you can give your students about the art of archery. We'll start with the more common, working our way to the more obscure.

QUIVER

A quiver is a container for holding arrows. Most look like a tube or long box, about 30 inches long by 6 to 8 inches across, with an opening at one end. They are commonly made from leather, but there are many other options available, such as cloth, plastic, and cardboard. Ancient archers used horn, wood, or even (in the case of Pacific Northwest natives) the hollowed out carcass of a dead beaver. As long as it will hold your arrows together and protect them, it will work.

Quivers can be worn on the back or hip. The hip quiver is convenient and easy to draw from; ancient medieval archers used hip quivers or simply carried their arrows in their hands. Robin Hood of Hollywood always uses the back quiver, but those didn't come into popularity until centuries after he was robbing from the rich and giving to the poor. Back quivers are better for walking through tall grass or brush, but the over-the-shoulder draw requires a little practice. Some versions have one strap; others have two like a backpack. Some back quivers designed for hunting have the hole in the bottom, and the arrows are stored point-up; plastic clips hold the arrows in place until they are needed.

back quiver

hip quiver

Ground quivers are ideal for beginning archery instruction. They are easy to operate, and keep the arrows in plain sight of the students and instructor so everyone can see when all the arrows have been shot. A ground quiver sits upon the firing line or is driven into the ground within reach of the archer. They range from elaborate wooden

boxes with score card clips and individual arrow holes to "ring quivers" made from a bent piece of steel rod.

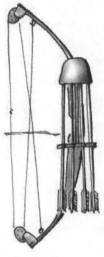

Bow quivers are typically seen only on compound bows used for hunting. They are basically a rack that bolts to the bow riser, with clips for holding a few hunting arrows. A rigid plastic pocket covers the razor-sharp broadheads for safety.

BRACERS

Sometimes referred to as "arm guards", the bracer is safety gear that should be required in all beginning archery programs (see the rant in the Teaching section). Although ancient peoples made them from things as diverse as feathers and ivory, today they are generally made from leather or plastic. The bracer straps to the inside of the archers left forearm (for right-

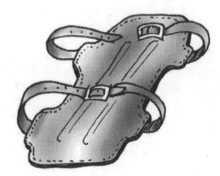

handed archers), and prevents the string from striking their forearm when their form isn't perfect. It also has the added benefit of helping to keep loose sleeves out of the path of the bowstring. In my classes, I make bracers optional for adults, but don't be fooled into thinking that "good" archers don't wear them- there is archaeological evidence of bracers being worn by some of the toughest archers in history, the Welsh longbowmen of the 14th century.

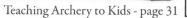

FINGERS

On heavier bows, it is nice to have something to protect your fingers from the bowstring. Three-fingered archery gloves, commonly called "fingers", cover an archer's drawing fingers to aid in smooth release and prevent blisters. They are generally not needed on bows less than 30 pounds, so I don't even tell younger students about them. Often, if kids see someone at the range using them, they complain if they don't have them

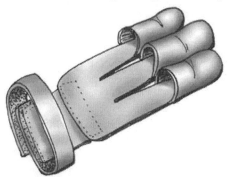

as well. But with the low draw weight and limited number of shots a beginning archer experiences, blisters are rarely a problem. The bigger problem stems from them trying to figure out how to grab the string when their fingers are covered up and they have no sense of touch...

If your fingers can stand it, shoot without gloves. The true practice of archery demands a close sympathy (so to speak) between the bowman and his weapons, reached only through the delicately-trained sense of touch.
-Maurice Thompson, 1878

TABS

An archery tab is a simple piece of leather or plastic that goes between an archers fingers and the bowstring. It usually has a hole or loop to put a finger through, so the tab doesn't land somewhere downrange upon release. They are inexpensive and easy to make, but their use is somehow totally baffling to young archers. Tabs fill the same need as *fingers*, so it might be wise to only introduce tabs to more advanced students.

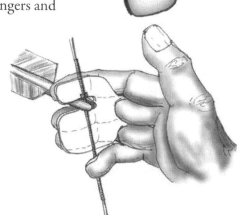

TARGET FACE

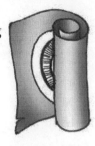

To aid in scoring, the target face gives archers something to shoot at. There are many versions available (and you can make up your own, as well) but the most common is five multicolored concentric circles. Animal silhouettes are also available; see the section on Crafts for additional information on making target faces.

TARGET BUTT

The target butt is a dense, fibrous mass designed to stop arrows effectively without breaking them. The cheapest butt is three straw bales stacked upon each other, and this works well for most introductory applications. When archers shoot higher poundage bows, though, you will start to see arrows passing all the way through, and you will have to move up to a more advanced butt, like self-healing foam. Traditional round butts of woven sisal rope are attractive, durable, and work exceptionally well. They are often mounted on a large wooden tripod that can be moved to different ranges. Their drawback is that they can be expensive and hard to find.

TARGET PINS

Made from bent wire or large-headed nails, target pins poke through the target face and into the butt, holding it in place.

MECHANICAL RELEASE

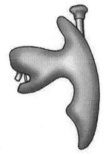

These come in many configurations, but all have the same function: they hold the string for the archer, releasing it upon command. Oftentimes, these release aids have a strap that goes around the wrist, leaving the hand free to operate a trigger very much like that on a gun. They give a very smooth release, increasing accuracy, so they're generally banned in tournaments- but used enthusiastically for hunting by all but the most traditional

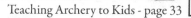

bowhunters. Another benefit is that with high-poundage compound bows, they protect your fingers better than tabs or gloves.

BOW REEL

A bow reel is basically a fishing reel that screws into the threaded ferrule on your hunting bow. It allows a bowfisherman to retrieve his arrow (and fish!) quickly and easily.

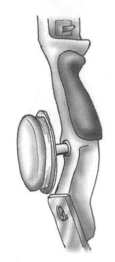

THUMB RING

This is a primitive but effective release aid used by Turkish archers since the middle ages. It gives the archer a way to hold the high draw weight of the Turkish composite bow without excessive pain, and allows for a cleaner release.

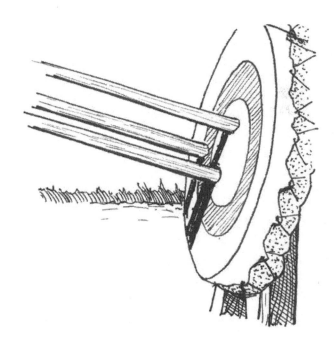

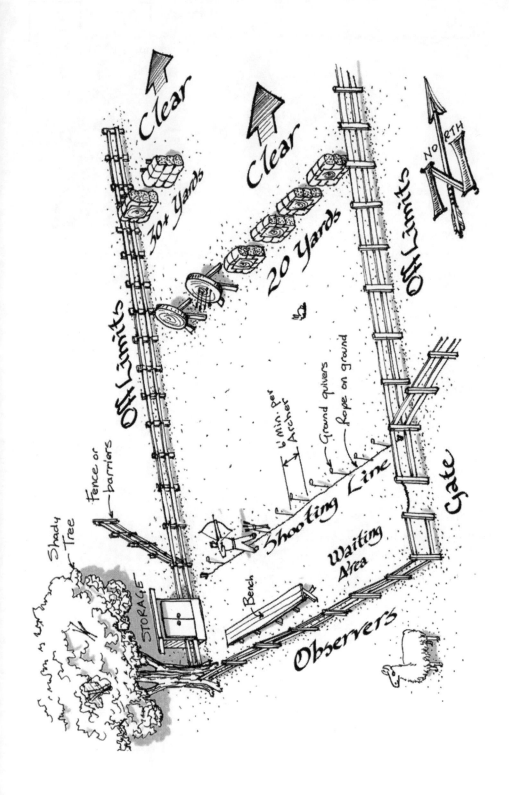

THE RANGE

SETTING UP THE RANGE

There are many different types of archery ranges. This section presents the basic physical requirements for an average instructional target shooting range. In reality, your actual range might look very different from this, depending on your site, program, budget, and other factors. The most important thing to consider when designing your range is safety. All ranges should have:

➤ Good visibility so the instructor can see everything that is going on

➤ A means to control access so bystanders (or archers) don't stumble into harm's way

➤ A system to control arrows that miss the target butts

As long as you cover these critical elements, with a little creativity you can make a safe archery range almost anywhere, even indoors. Once your archers are more experienced, you can get a lot more flexible with what a range looks like, and expose them to field archery (more about that in the section on Activities) and other archery games outside of the range. Although you could shoot archery anywhere, a properly set up range will help you maintain safety with beginning archers and eliminate distractions so they can focus on practicing the basic skills. Let's talk about the range, and its different components.

Site

Any large, open space will do for a range, but the best sites are relatively flat and free of obstructions. The size of your site will depend largely on how many target butts you have, and what distances you want to shoot at. A good basic width for the range should be about 6 feet per archer with an extra 6 feet per side, so if you were planning to shoot 8 archers at once, you'd want a 60 foot wide piece of ground [(8 archers x 6 feet) + (2 x 6 feet per side]. The minimum length of the range should be the shooting distance, plus 6 feet for butts and 15 feet for the waiting area behind the line. Therefore, if you wanted to shoot at 30 yards (90 feet), you'd need 111 feet of length [90 feet+ 6 feet+ 15 feet]. By these formulae, a range for younger archers with only 20-yard (60 feet) targets would need to be 81 feet long. Bear in mind that these sizes are minimums, and a little extra space is always good. We've also not yet included off-limits areas or clear areas behind.

Shooting distances are traditionally given in yards and sometimes

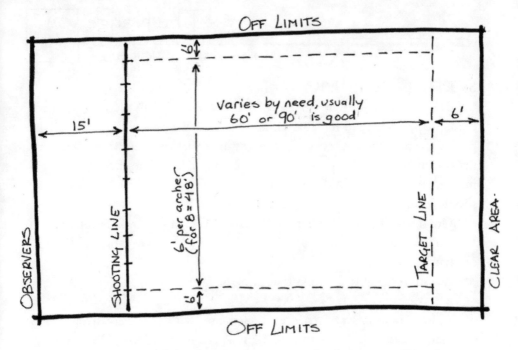

OFF LIMITS

OFF LIMITS

6'

Varies by need, usually
60' or 90' is good

6'

15'

6' per archer
(for 8 = 48')

OBSERVERS

SHOOTING LINE

TARGET LINE

CLEAR AREA.

meters for the metrically inclined. Distances in the diagrams will be shown in feet because most American tape measures are printed in feet.

If possible, orient your range so that the archers are shooting towards the north (or south, if your range is in the southern hemisphere). This will keep the sun out of their faces and on the targets throughout the day. The grass should be mowed low so that arrows are easier to find and retrieve. A few trees or a sun tarp by the waiting area would be a nice addition, to provide shade.

As an alternate, a range can be set up indoors. These ranges can be smaller, because the building enclosure replaces the off-limits area to the side and the clear area behind. Indoor ranges need some sort of special backstop behind the target butts, such as a tightly woven net or dense padding on the back wall, to keep arrows from being broken or the building from being damaged. Nowadays, indoor public ranges are more common than outdoor ones, and they are usually attached to pro shops that sell archery equipment. Shooting indoors has the advantage that you are protected from cold, rainy, or windy weather, but it also takes away some of the magic of being in the woods and fields with your bow in hand.

Eventually, when your archers are more skilled, they can shoot places besides the range. The section on Activities has examples of appropriate off-range shooting, as well a discussion about the special safety precautions needed.

Storage

Although you can take the archery equipment away with you at the end of each day, in most institutional settings it's easier if you have some provision for on-site storage. An archery locker (called an Ascham, if you're really in-the-know) doesn't have to be very big to hold plenty of equipment for a dozen people. A shed 3 feet by 6 feet by 7 feet tall would do the trick nicely. It should be weather proof, rodent proof (strings and feathers are particularly tasty to mice), and most importantly, it should have a secure lock to which only the instructor and a supervisor have the key. Unsecured archery equipment is a magnet for trouble, drawing in curious students (and occasionally staff members) eager to try out their new archery skills when you aren't around.

Waiting area

Oftentimes, you will have more archers in a class than you can safely handle on the shooting line at once. This makes a little more workload for you, but is an opportunity for those not shooting to get a little rest and watch others shoot, and maybe even learn from their mistakes. A waiting area with a bench or some seats should be about five yards back from the shooting line, so archers on the line don't feel crowded, and you have room to move behind the archers as you are watching their progress and giving advice. The waiting area should, however, be inside the fence or barrier of the range; this keeps those waiting from wandering off, and eager observers from entering your class without you knowing.

Shooting line

The shooting line is the reference point from which the range is laid out. Anything in front of it (towards the butts) is the danger zone, and anything behind it is a safe area. When archers are shooting, they should be straddling the line, with one foot on each side. This guarantees that no one can be in front of anyone else. Your shooting line can be paint or chalk on the ground, but what seems to work best is a long piece of thick, brightly colored rope. If you stake it down at each end and pull it tight, it will be both straight and permanent. Poly rope works best for this, because it doesn't rot with extended exposure to moisture and bright sunlight.

Target butts

There is a description of target butts in the section on Equipment. The simplest butts are made from three hay bales stacked on top of each other. It sometimes helps to drive a pair of wooden poles into the ground behind the butts, and tie the whole assembly together with baling twine to prevent it from moving. Regardless of how the butts are made, be sure that they are secure and won't fall over in the wind or when hit. The sound of a dozen arrows breaking under a toppling target butt is unsettling, to say the least.

Barriers and fences

The range can be a dangerous place, and it's critical that you have a way to keep unknowing people from accidentally stumbling into harm's way. Ideally, there should be a fence around the entire range, with a gate where you can see who is coming and going. In reality, that doesn't often exist, so at a minimum, you need an impassible barrier along the sides of your range, extending from the shooting line well into the clear area. The construction of your barrier should be appropriate to the sort of people who will be near your range; if it's only adults, then a brightly colored "DO NOT CROSS" tape might be enough. For younger crowds, a split-rail fence or something that will physically stop them would be better. And if there are toddlers and the very young, you will probably need a chain link fence, wall, chicken wire, or something that goes all the way down to the ground.

Observation area

People just love to watch archery. Your range should have a designated area for spectators, not just so you can be a good ambassador of archery, but also so you can keep an eye on the safety of the bystanders. The best place for observers is outside the range, behind the shooting line and waiting area. Making chairs or benches available, as well as shade and water, would be a nice touch if you have the means.

Off-limits area

With beginning archers, it occasionally happens that they shoot VERY wide of the target, and if they are already aiming at the outside targets, then they might shoot out of the range entirely. So, you need to have empty space on either side of your range that is off-limits while the range is in use. This space should be wider as you get closer to the target butts, and doesn't need to be much wider than the range itself at the shooting line. If the natural layout of your range already makes it so people can't be in the off-limits area (if you're next to a lake, for example) then that's even better.

To make a hunting arrow requires about an hour, and one should be willing to look for one almost this time when it is lost.
  -Dr. Saxton Pope, 1923

Clear area

When laying out a range, the clear area is probably the single most important consideration. Behind the butts, you need a clear area for all those arrows your students will be shooting over the tops of the butts. And I am talking about a LOT of arrows when they are beginners. For a 30 yard range and students using 25 pound bows, you will need at least another 30 yards clear behind the targets. Heavier bows will demand much more. If you have any doubt about the size of your clear area behind, take the heaviest bow you are going to use and shoot an arrow over the top of the butts to test it. Keep shooting arrows progressively higher, until you know how far the worst miss will go. To be extra safe, make sure that even the space *beyond* your clear area will also be empty of people or breakable equipment.

You can make your clear area a lot smaller if you have a helpful natural feature. A hill or embankment makes the perfect backstop because if it's high enough, it can make your clear area very short. Also, getting your arrows out of a hillside is a breeze. A forest can be a good backdrop, but it makes collecting arrows much more difficult. And beware of toxic plants- I once taught at a range with a forested backdrop, and spent much of the summer covered in poison oak blisters. A lake can be an acceptable clear area, but you should try to have ten or twenty yards between the butts and the lake to catch the near misses, or you will spend a lot of time wading out to get arrows. Finally, as a last resort, you can have a "hard backstop" instead of a clear area. This could be manmade, like a padded wall or a net suspended from poles; or natural, like a cliff face. If possible, hard backstops should catch the arrows gently, so they don't break or bounce back towards the archers.

RUNNING THE RANGE

Once you've set up a safe range, you're halfway done. Then next step is to run it safely when archers are present. Running the range safely is mostly a matter of common sense and communication. It also helps to have a mental picture of how you and your students will use the range; spend some time trying to anticipate things that could go wrong, and prepare for them in advance. Read through Sample Lesson #2 in the Teaching section to see an example of how the range is used during a lesson. As long as the students are paying attention to you, and you to them, things should go smoothly.

The Four Basic Rules

You could make a long list of regulations for the range, but I find it easier for students to remember a few concise, all-encompassing rules. On my range, the Four Basic Rules are:

1. Wait until the instructor gives permission before you do anything.
2. Point arrows only at the ground or the targets.
3. Be aware of your surroundings at all times.
4. Have fun.

These easy-to-remember rules cover the most critical areas of range safety, and must be firmly embedded in the minds of your students, so repeat them often. Rule number one is important and widely applicable, a critical tool for ensuring range safety. In general, without your approval the students shouldn't pick up any equipment, move to the firing line, load arrows, shoot, retrieve arrows... you get the picture.

Other rules

There are also other range rules that are more informational, and could be explained to the students and/or posted on a sign, but don't warrant repeated review. Some are simply elaborations of the Four Basic Rules. If you incorporate these concepts into your teaching, then you might not even need to list them out:

➤ Stay in the waiting area when it's not your turn to shoot.

➤ If you notice a damaged arrow or bow, tell the instructor.

➤ Archers should always stand with one foot on either side of the shooting line when shooting. This guarantees that no one can get too far forward or behind other archers, putting them in danger of being shot.

➤ Stop shooting if you see anyone downrange, and tell the instructor immediately.

➤ If an arrow should be dropped or flip off of the bow, the archer may only reload and shoot it if they can touch it with their bow. (This old archery tradition is a good rule to follow, but don't let it get out of hand; if the student has to do wild contortions or get in front of other shooters, then count that arrow as shot.)

➤ It's considered rude to make noises or talk to other archers while they are aiming. A little talk in between shots is OK, but not if it slows down the shooting or annoys others.

Modify these rules when needed to suit your specific range, equipment, and situation. You can also make up additional rules that are specific to your range and teaching environment, but try to keep to just a few that are basic and all-encompassing. The best rules are positive in nature and stay away from the word "don't". For example, it is better to say "point arrows only at the ground or the targets" than to say "don't point arrows at people or animals." But remember, the more rules there are, the harder it is to remember them. You can often avoid making a lot of extra rules if you explain things thoroughly during your teaching.

SAMPLE INVENTORY FOR A CAMP PROGRAM

To run a safe and effective camp archery program, you don't need a lot of fancy gear. The following equipment list is for a summer camp program that can handle up to 16 archers per hour, if the program is running efficiently. If your program is larger or smaller, you can adjust the quantities accordingly. Start by acquiring equipment in the *required* category, then if you have the means, get what you can from the *strongly recommended* category. Collect items from the *helpful* category as money, time, and opportunity allow. You might also need other special equipment not shown if you plan on repairing your own equipment or are going to teach specialty programs, such as making arrows. Required supplies for these activities are listed in the section on Crafts.

Required equipment

Qty.	Item	Notes & Description
8	Bows	With strings. Draw length & weight will vary by archer size & age; see table on next page. One or two should be left-handed or have a shelf on both sides.
4 doz. (minimum)	Arrows	Length and spine weight matched to bows, 26" is a good length for most camp programs
8	Ground quivers	You can make these from bent wire if funds are low
8	Bracers	Appropriately sized for archers
4	Target butts	Two archers can share a butt with little difficulty.
50'	Rope	Yellow synthetic, for shooting line
varies	Stakes, cord, fencing, etc.	To create safety zones around the range as described earlier in this chapter

Strongly recommended equipment

Qty.	Item	Notes & Description
4 doz. more	Arrows	You are going to lose or break a great many arrows with novice archers. Less replacement arrows will be needed with more skilled archers, or shorter programs
8	Target faces	You can make your own if funding is tight
32	Target pins	You can make these too
8 more	Bracers	So archers in the waiting area can get ready, saving time
2 or 3	Bows	In different sizes than your main equipment, both smaller and larger, for special archers
Several	Bowstrings	Properly sized for bows, to replace worn strings.
Extra	Everything listed in the "required" section	For replacing things as they get damaged or wear out

Helpful additional equipment

Qty.	Item	Notes & Description
4 more	Target butts & faces	If you want your archers to each have their own to shoot at
Some	Nock point markers	See section on equipment repair
Some	Arrow repair equipment	See section on equipment repair
Some	Markers, paper, etc.	For making targets, posters, visual aids, etc.

A note on bow weight

It is better to have bows that are too light than too heavy, as they can still be used in a pinch. A very loose guideline chart for bow weight is printed below, but is only for equipment planning purposes. DO NOT let any of your students see it, or they might get the false idea that they should be able to pull a bow of a certain weight, causing them to use a bow that's too heavy for them. Use your best judgment to match each archer to their proper bow weight.

Draw Weight	Girls/ Women	Boys/ Men
15# or less	8-12 years	8-10 years
20-25#	10-16 years	10-14 years
30-35#	14+ years	12-16 years
40-45#	16+ years	14+ years
50-55#	Not many	16+ years
60# +	Very rare	Not many

All other things
being equal,
it is the man who
shoots with his
heart in his bow
that hits the mark.
~Saxton Pope

PREPARATION

TEACHING PRIORITIES

When teaching archery to kids, it helps to keep in mind your priorities. Here they are, in order from most important to least important:

➤ Safety
➤ Fun
➤ Learning
➤ Improvement
➤ Achievement

SAFETY

In any archery program, especially one involving kids, safety should be the first concern. We can break this down into two areas: keeping archers from hurting others, and protecting archers from hurting themselves. Archery is a safe sport when common sense and order are followed, but chaos and carelessness can instantly provide a chance for someone to get hurt.

There are organizational tools to help you keep young archers and innocent bystanders safe. The first line of defense is to set up the range correctly, so that there will never be anyone downrange of archers while they are shooting. Refer to the section on The Range for a diagram of a typical safe archery range.

Someone should act as a range warden. This person is responsible for watching the range, and stopping the shooting if a dangerous situation develops, such as someone accidentally walking into the area beyond the targets. In smaller programs, this job can be done by the instructor. It just means that you have to have eyes in the back of your head.

Bystanders should have a safe watching area that is behind the shooting line, and ropes or some sort of barrier should prevent anyone from entering the range anywhere except behind the firing line. A waiting area should be available for those who are not shooting, at least 5 to 10 yards away from the active archers.

The most significant danger young archers pose is to themselves. In the first session with a new group of students, I like to point out that no one is likely to get killed by target arrows and 20-pound bows, but that does not make them toys. Many other gruesome possibilities besides death await someone unfortunate enough to be struck by a target arrow: a welt the size of a softball, a broken tooth, or a lost eye. Here are some common dangers to look out for:

➻ Obviously, roughhousing and archery don't mix. Running isn't allowed anywhere on the range, especially with arrows. If archers trip, they could fall on their arrows and skewer themselves.

➻ Use caution when walking towards the targets. Kids are always excited to see how well they've done, but the nocks of the arrows are just as dangerous to the eye as the point. If you trip just before you reach the target, you could land face-first into the bristling arrows in the bullseye.

➻ Use arrows that are long enough to avoid draw-through. If a long-armed archer draws their arrow past the shelf of the bow, the point could come to rest against the belly (inside) of the bow. Then, when they release the string, the force of the bow could violently smash the arrow between the bow and the string, shattering it and forcing splinters to go everywhere, including into the archer's forearm.

➻ Archers should not talk to each other or bystanders while on the shooting line. People tend to turn towards those with whom they are speaking, pointing their bow in the same direction.

➻ No archery equipment should be within reach anywhere except on the shooting line. This especially important with younger kids. You can monitor the equipment if it's on the line, and watch for mischief.

➻ Make sure all equipment is properly sized and maintained in good working order. The first half of the Crafts section has more on maintenance and repair.

Of course, there are exceptions to most rules, and sometimes you just have to use common sense: on a field archery course, for example, archers will constantly have their bows and arrows in front of or behind a shooting line, but there are additional safety protocols in place to balance this and keep it safe. At times like this, you must weigh the skill level, maturity, and number of your students against your experience level, shooting environment, and available help.

FUN

In 99 out of 100 cases, that is why the archers are here. You don't have to make archery fun; movies, fairy tales, stories, and art have already done that for you. These kids really want to be archers. Your job is to keep archery fun. Here are several fun-destroyers, and how to avoid them:

Pain: Kids hate pain. Unfortunately, many would-be archers are put off of archery forever because they were slapped by a bowstring on the forearm

at a young age. Next to overall safety, I make preventing bowstring slap my second highest priority, above all else. Make every kid wear a bracer, and teach them the slap-avoidance techniques explained towards the end of the Teaching section. In addition to string slap, a second source of pain is sore fingers. For short sessions, this will only be a minor irritation, and will go away quickly after they stop shooting. For longer sessions, consider providing tabs or fingers.

Boredom: This varies by age group, with the younger ones needing more change more often. On the second or third lesson, I start introducing novelty targets, archery games, etc. and add more variety each time they return. Some older archers might only be interested in perfecting their technique on a regular target face, but it's the exception rather than the rule. You can allow these archers to continue with a regular target, or if you have several of them, set up a special practice session just for them.

Insecurity: Many newcomers are nervous about their skill level, and the competitive nature of sports puts a high demand on their self esteem. Speak encouraging words and celebrate accomplishments. If a student does poorly, help them by offering a little advice as well as pointing out the things they did right. Also, be careful to make your goals appropriate for the skill level of your students. Shooting soda cans off of stumps at twenty yards is great for 15-year olds, but would cause frustration and resentment in most 10-year olds.

Fear: This comes from the unknown. Explain everything carefully and slowly before you do it, and make sure that your students are "with you" as you go. Fear disappears quickly once students understand what's going on. So, keep it fun. It's what keeps them coming back, and recruiting friends. Some day, these kids will be the ones carrying the torch of Archery when we are gone.

LEARNING

Most people are smart enough to figure out the rough basics of archery by themselves. But it's the job of you, the instructor, to help them learn more information faster then they could by themselves, while keeping them from injuring themselves or wasting too much time going down the wrong path. The knowledge and experience level of instructors varies widely, but it is pretty likely that you know more than the kids. Do your best to educate yourself about archery, so you in turn can educate them. If a student asks a question you don't know the answer too, admit your ignorance and promise to find the answer and give it to them at the next lesson. This collective learning process is enriching for everyone. Besides this book you are holding, there are lots of archery resources available, both online and in print. See the Resource section in the back of this book for ideas.

IMPROVEMENT

With only a small amount of practice, this goal is readily achieved by most students. Kids who couldn't hit the broad side of a barn (literally) can often get at least one or two arrows in the center rings after a few sessions. The important thing here is to look at improvement relative to where the student started, and not at their performance compared to their neighbors. Sometimes, recording scores over several sessions will give a tangible way for the student to see their improvement. Be careful, though, of beginners luck. Some archers take a long time to get back to the scores they shot before they started to "learn something". This can be demoralizing, but sometimes older kids will be more understanding if you explain the Learning Curve to them.

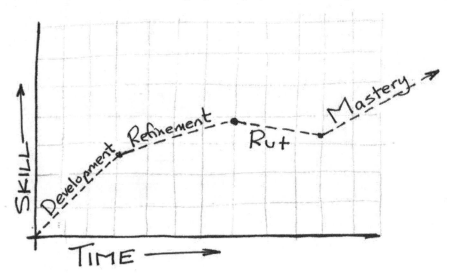

It basically has four phases:

➥ Rapid Development: The learner is gaining skills rapidly, and each time there is a noticeable improvement, especially compared with their starting skill level.

➥ Skill Refinement: The learner has a handle on the basic skills, and is now refining and improving the details. This might include finding

a stable anchor point and stance, as well as increasing muscle tone. Improvement here is slower, but the student is skilled enough now to still appreciate the improvements.

➡ The "Rut": The learner, confident with the skill refinement stage, begins to experiment with variations on the things they've learned. This is sometimes coupled with carelessness, either out of complacency or overconfidence. Unfortunately, this dip often occurs at the same time the learner is in danger of getting bored with the skill. It's important to encourage archers to hang in there, to get to the next phase...

➡ Mastery: After all the experimentation, practice, and gauging the right confidence level, the learner is at a point where they have control of all the skills and can perform well.

The phases often repeat themselves in a cycle. As an instructor, it's important to know your students, and to spot when someone is in a rut and struggling. Explain to them what's going on, and give them gentle objective advice and point out things that they might not be seeing due to their situation.

ACHIEVEMENT

This is the least important concern for teaching archery to kids. At younger ages, whether or not they can get high scores is pretty irrelevant. What is important at this age is instilling a love of archery, and giving them the basic skills to take it further if they chose. Unfortunately, scores and achievement are the easiest goals to measure. Sometimes parents and other kids will become overly interested in achievement of this type, but at this level, the best answer is to increase your focus on the other areas like fun and improvement.

For older kids, achievement might become more of a priority, especially if they are interested in some day competing. These kids will generally use their own scores to motivate themselves, without the interference of you or parents. Allow them to do this, but don't let them lose sight of the other four priority items.

Equipment Selection & Preparation

If you're new to archery, the wide array of specialized and archaic equipment might seem daunting at first. You can simplify it in your mind by concentrating on the two essential items, the bow and arrow, and learning about the rest as you go.

ARROW SELECTION

For an in-depth look at arrows, flip to "The Arrow" in the Equipment section. There you can learn about materials, designs, and all the parts of the arrow. But for starters, suffice it to say that the arrow is just a very straight stick that flies to the target. As the archery instructor, there are three factors in arrows you should be immediately concerned with: arrow length, spine weight, and damage.

Arrow length

Each archer has an arrow length that is correct for their draw. An arrow of the proper length will protrude about an inch past the back of the bow at full draw. If it's longer, the arrow will have undesirable flight characteristics. If it's shorter, the archer risks overdrawing the arrow and getting hurt. An archer's draw length can be accurately measured with a special arrow that is extra long, without fletchings, and marked in one-inch increments. The archer simply draws it, and an observer notes what length is indicated just beyond the back of the bow. A second method, requiring no special tools, is for the archer to put a yardstick against the base of their throat and bring their outstretched arms together in front, around the stick as shown below. The position of the fingertips on the yardstick indicates the correct arrow length.

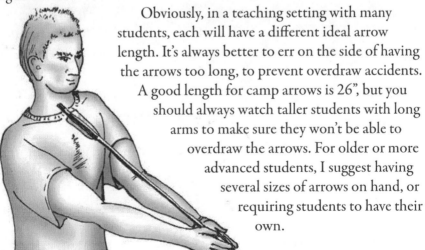

Obviously, in a teaching setting with many students, each will have a different ideal arrow length. It's always better to err on the side of having the arrows too long, to prevent overdraw accidents. A good length for camp arrows is 26", but you should always watch taller students with long arms to make sure they won't be able to overdraw the arrows. For older or more advanced students, I suggest having several sizes of arrows on hand, or requiring students to have their own.

PREPARATION

When you take a longer shaft than your own... this way pulleth the bow asunder, and then the bow flyeth in many pieces.
-Roger Ascham, 1545

Spine weight

Arrows are designed to be matched to a bow of a certain weight for optimum shooting results. The *spine weight* is a relative measure of the arrow's stiffness, and should be within five pounds of the draw weight of the bow. You can shoot an arrow with a spine weight greatly different than the draw weight of the bow, but your arrow will erroneously shoot left or right of the target. For a further (and more complicated) explanation of this phenomenon, see the section on Archer's Paradox in the Lore section. Institutional wood arrows are often marked with the spine weight right on the shaft, but for other arrows such as aluminum shafts, you have to look at a code number on the label and cross-reference it against the shaft length on a spine weights table from the manufacturer.

As a side note, shooting an arrow with a spine weight lower than the draw weight of the bow does not normally mean that the arrow is too weak to be shot from the bow safely; it just means that the arrow is too flexible to be shot accurately.

Damage

A damaged arrow is a danger to archer and bystander alike, as the powerful forces that build up in the shooting process could cause it to break, fly off in an unintended direction, or both. As instructor, you will need to inspect your arrows prior to each class, looking for cracked shafts, loose points, split nocks, and missing fletchings. Encourage your archers to look at their arrows as well, and bring any they think are damaged to your attention. This will help them learn more about the process, as well as helping you handle the safety burden.

Any damaged arrows should be immediately set aside where they won't be accidentally used. After the class, you can sort through your damaged arrows and decide which should be completely destroyed and which are salvageable, based on your skill and comfort level with arrow repair. Incidentally, I recommend that you destroy all irreparably damaged arrows, so they don't accidentally get put back in with the good ones. Simply throwing them away is not good enough; curious kids will see them in the trash and pull them out to play with them when you're not around, possibly getting hurt in the process. One idea for disposing of damaged arrows is to save them up and have a ceremonial campfire where they are honorably retired into the flames, in respect for their good service.

If you cover only these three aspects of arrow selection, you have done your duty to protect the safety of your students. If you want to go beyond this minimum, then you will need to look into other factors, such as shaft material, fletching design, etc. Other sections of this book have more specific information on arrow selection; you can read about the merits of fletching styles in the Equipment section, and spine weight in the Lore section.

BOW SELECTION

Much like arrows, bows can be a complicated subject. For an in-depth look at bows, flip to "The Bow" in the Equipment section . Keep in mind that a bow is just a bent stick for throwing arrows. To get started, you only need to understand three things about bows: draw weight, draw length, and damage.

Draw weight

All bows are labeled showing draw length and draw weight; it looks something like this: 24# @ 28". It is usually written or printed on the belly of the upper riser. The first number is the draw weight at full draw, in this case twenty-four pounds when pulled back to twenty-eight inches. It's important to match the right bow to each archer; a bow that it too heavy will be difficult to pull and impossible to aim correctly. Generally speaking, the archer should be able to pull the bow back and hold it at full draw for several seconds without shaking. A bow that is too light will be very easy to draw and shoot, but will not perform as well as a heavier bow, and might get frustrating to the student after a while. This is a lesser problem than the bow that is too heavy. In that case, the student won't be able to aim properly, and will start to develop bad habits like shooting too quickly or not using the proper form. In extreme cases, a bow that is too heavy can cause excessive muscle fatigue and soreness.

There is a chart at the end of The Range section that you can use to estimate bow weights when purchasing them for groups, but don't even sneak a peek at it when you're matching bows to students.

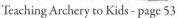

Draw length

Remember that label on the upper limb that we looked at before? The second number is the draw length. This is the farthest the bow should be drawn. On low-weight fiberglass bows like most camp equipment, overdrawing the bow a little will only make the draw weight stack up, with no real danger. But on laminated or wooden bows, overdrawing only an inch or two can be disastrous and cause the bow to crack or even explode. If you have tall or long-armed students, have them test draw several times with an arrow of a known length (or a measuring arrow with inches marked on it) to make sure they don't draw farther than the bow can support.

Under-drawing is less of a concern, and will simply mean that the full draw weight of the bow will not be developed.

A bow full drawn is seven-eighths broken.
-Thomas Waring, 1832

Damage

When a bow is bent at full draw, it's straining to use every fiber of its being to whip the arrow towards the target. Any additional stress (such as overdrawing) could push it past its limit. So now imagine if that bow were cracked. If it lost, say, one eighth of its capacity, then pulling it would use up the rest and SMASH! you'd have pieces everywhere. And maybe crying kids. So, inspect all your bows before each class. Look for cracks on both the back and belly, frayed strings (especially at the servings and nock loops), and loose hardware. Any suspicious bows should be put out of service immediately, pending a more thorough investigation.

It's no coincidence that arrows and bows have basically the same three things to look out for: proper length, proper weight, and damage. You need to be keeping a constant eye out for all of them any time you are at the range.

PREPARATION

STRINGING THE BOWS

Once you've inspected the bows, you are ready to string them for the day's work. The easiest and safest way to do this is with a *bow stringer*, a length of sturdy cord with pockets at each end. These pockets are slipped over the ends of the bow, and the bowstring is put into one of the string nocks. Then, you step on the bow stringer while pulling up on the bow by the handle, belly-side down (see illustration). When you get the bow up high enough, you can slip the second loop of the bowstring into the other string nock. Let the bow back down and remove the bow stringer. Check to be sure the string is securely seated at both ends of the bow, and you're ready to shoot.

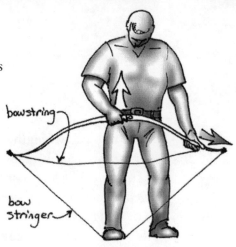

A second, trickier method can be used on lighter bows, and doesn't require a bow stringer. With a little practice, you can even use it on heavy longows. With your right hand, grasp the bow by the handle, with the belly facing away from you (backwards). Make sure the string is already in the bottom nock, and then place the bottom tip of the bow against the inside of your right foot. Place your left palm against the upper limb, with your fingers wrapped around between the string and the bow. Simultaneously pull with your right hand and press with your left, bending the bow away from you. As the bow bends, slide your left hand away from you and up the bow, until you get to the string nock. The string follows your fingers up the bow, and then drops into place in the string nock. Again, once the bow is strung, check both ends to make sure the string is securely in place.

When you string a bow you are unfamiliar with, or purchase a new string for an existing bow, it's a good idea to check the *fistmele*, or brace height. This is the distance between the string and the inside of the bow's handle. It's not often listed, so you have to depend on having the correct

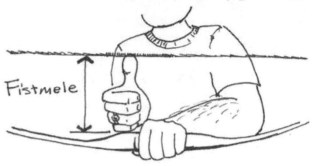

Fistmele

length bowstring to get the right fistmele for your bow. A quick method to see if you're close, and the only way to check it on bows with adjustable strings, is to measure it in the ancient medieval way: make a fist and place the bottom of it on the inside of the handle. Stick out your thumb out in the "thumbs up!" gesture, and you should just barely be able to touch the bowstring with your thumb tip. If the distance is much farther than that, you probably have too short a string and you could dangerously overdraw the bow if you pull it. If the distance is much less, your string is too long and the bow will vibrate uncomfortably with every shot. You can make minor adjustments in fistmele by twisting the bowstring; more twist makes the string slightly shorter and will increase the fistmele.

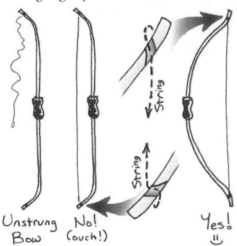

Unstrung Bow

No! (ouch!)

String

String

Yes!

Occasionally a beginner will mistakenly string a recurve bow backwards. This is could damage fiberglass bows, and will destroy wooden ones. The best way to make sure you've strung the bow the right direction is to look at the string nocks; the string should smoothly follow the angle of the nock.

At the close of the day's shooting, you will need to unstring the bows. The process is the same as stringing, but in reverse. Storing bows unstrung prevents them from becoming weak and permanently bent. Compound bows are the exception to this rule, for two reasons. First, due to the cables and pulleys that give them their speed, they can't be unstrung without special equipment. Second, they are made from modern materials that do not weaken when left under stress. If you are using compound bows, store them as they are without worry of damaging them.

That instant of time
in which the sight
suddenly concentrates itself
upon the target's center,
whilst every other object
grows dark and indistinct,
is the critical moment
of your aim.

~Maurice Thompson

Tell me how to do it, I will remember for an hour. Show me how to do it, I will remember for a day. Allow me to do it myself, I will remember for a lifetime.
-old teaching adage

TEACHING KIDS TO SHOOT

That's what this book is all about, isn't it? Teaching can be somewhat intimidating at first; all those faces eagerly watching, expecting you to know everything. It's your job to pass all this knowledge on to them. You can do it! The first step is to

Once you've got that part under control, then you can get down to the business of teaching. Here are a few general ideas to get you started:

Organize & prepare

Preparation is really important, and happens on many levels. Before your first class ever shows up, you should make sure you've examined all the equipment, thought about your lessons, ordered supplies, and prepared for every contingency you can think of. Reading this book would also be a good way to prepare! Preparation goes hand-in-hand with organization. After you inventory your equipment, find a place for everything and make sure you can get to it quickly. After you prepare your lesson, write it down and put it somewhere you won't lose it.

KISS (Keep It Simple, Silly!)

Take everything one step at a time, both with your students, and with yourself. Teach fundamentals first, and save the tricky stuff for follow-up lessons. Nine-year-olds do not need to know how to use an illuminated vernier sight, even if you do have one and are dying to show them. It will just confuse and frustrate them.

If things get too complicated, break them apart into smaller teaching tasks. You don't need to demand that all seven parts of the shot are done correctly; pick one area for a student to work on, and when they've got that under control, move on to another.

TEACHING

Constructive criticism techniques

Some people accept advice (read: criticism) more gracefully than others. It's your job as instructor to provide helpful criticism to anyone who is not perfect, and that will usually be everyone. Too much criticism, though, will leave a student feeling frustrated. Start your discussion by pointing out something the student is doing right, before you point out areas they need to improve. Finish your discussion with more recognition of their accomplishments. This leaves them in an open attitude, and helps them pay attention to the criticism.

Learning overload

There is a limit to how much a person can learn at one time and it varies by individual. Try not to give too much coaching all at once; pick one or two key items that are the most critical, and ask the student to concentrate on those. Next time, if those items have improved, pick one or two new items and gradually increase the list as the archer's skill progresses.

Keep it interesting

If you will be teaching the same group of kids many times, make sure you keep their interest level up by changing something in each day's shooting. Use different targets, play archery games, or ask the kids what they want to do today. Fixed-distance range shooting becomes stagnant quickly for young archers.

Superior archers

The goal of coaching any sport is for the student to become better than the instructor, so that over many generations, society can advance to greater and greater achievements. Occasionally, you will get a student that is a better archer than you are. Take advantage of this opportunity: use the student to demonstrate technique to others, and try to observe their strengths so you can teach them to everyone else. And don't forget: you don't need to be better than they are to continue coaching them. Even if you were entirely unable to draw a bow yourself, your knowledge of archery and your ability to identify good and bad technique would allow you to help archers of any level.

Now, we're ready to talk about how to shoot a bow.

Blindly direct your arrow by your sense of feeling. Let go the string.
-Maurice Thompson, 1878

OVERVIEW OF THE SHOOTING PROCESS

There are seven[1] basic steps to shooting archery— that sounds like a lot, but it all becomes automatic pretty quickly. We'll discuss each step and explain what's going on, so you can better teach it to others. All of the examples here are right handed, so you will need to reverse left and right in the directions for a left-handed archer. The steps are:

1. Stance
2. Load
3. Draw
4. Anchor
5. Aim
6. Release
7. Follow through

TEACHING

1. STANCE

The best stance is a comfortable one that can be maintained without great effort. Each archer will need to experiment with different variations until they discover one that is right for their body shape and shooting style, but everyone can start with the basics. Stand with feet shoulder-width apart and turn so that you can draw an imaginary line through the tips of the toes, right into the center of the target. Right-handed archers will stand so the target is to their left, and they will look over their left shoulders to shoot.

---

1.   According to Ascham, there are five steps to a good shot: Stand, Nock (load), Draw, Hold, and Loose (release). This is still a good system today, nearly 500 years after he wrote it. But when teaching beginners, it's good to put extra emphasis on "aim"; Ascham's students were soldiers being trained to fire volleys into large opposing armies, when aiming might not have been so important. "Follow through" is a modern concept appearing in most sporting endeavors, and likely would not have been known to him in these terms.

There are variations on this stance, such as the *open stance*. Here, you line up your feet as with the basic stance, then slide your leading foot backwards a little, so you face the target more. This stance is handy for longbow users and women with large busts, as it offers more string clearance. A *closed stance* is just the opposite, with your leading foot a little forward, so you are sort of shooting over your shoulder. There are also specialty stances, such as kneeling and prone, but those should be avoided in beginning classes.

2. LOADING THE BOW

The arrow goes on the bow so that the nock is fit to the string just beneath the nocking point indicator, with the index feather towards the

shooter. The shaft of the arrow should be on the same side of the bow as the shooter's arm, resting gently on the shelf or arrow rest. Though there are several ways to get the arrow from your quiver to the bow, the easiest method for novices is described in the sample lesson. In no case should your left hand ever have to leave the handle of the bow.

Grip types: string hand

Throughout history, there have been several ways mankind has drawn the bow. We'll talk about a few of them, but the most popular today is the basic three-fingered draw. It uses the index, middle, and ring finger to grip the string, with the string crossing these fingers between the very tip and the first joint of each. The arrow fits to the string between the index and middle fingers. Your hand is open and flat, curving only at the finger tips, and the palm of your hand opens towards your face. To release, you let your fingers relax until the string slips crisply from your grasp. This is the easiest grip to teach and by far the most common.

A slight variation on the traditional three-fingered grip is to use all three fingers placed under the arrow. This only works if you have a nocking point indicator affixed to the string; and on shorter bows, might cause excessive pinching of the ring finger. Avoid teaching this grip to kids.

In medieval Europe, the professional soldier-archers preferred a two-finger draw, and you still see it occasionally today. It's similar to the basic grip, but uses only the index and middle fingers. Eliminating the ring finger reduces pinching, makes the string have a more even follow from top to bottom, and provides for a crisper release. However, it requires much greater strength in the fingers, and can't be performed by most people on any but the lightest of bows. It was abandoned in favor of the three-fingered release in the mid-1500s.[2]

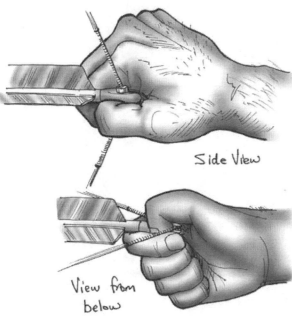

Side View

View from below

In central Asia, the *Mongolian release* prevailed for centuries. The hand is held palm down, and the thumb is hooked around the string at the first joint, with the arrow above it. The index finger is then latched over the thumb, creating a sort of mechanical lock. To release, the index finger is opened, and the thumb snaps open under string pressure. It allows the crispest release of all, as it has the least contact with the string. But the pressure built up on the thumb required Asiatic archers to use special rings to protect

TEACHING

---

2. As described by Ascham.

their thumb from the string. This is a really tricky style, and not for the inexperienced.

As an interesting side note, the Yahi (a Native American tribe on the other side of the planet) developed a variation of this technique as well[3]. However, the relatively low poundage of their bows made the thumb ring unnecessary.

Grip: bow hand

Right-handed shooters will grab the bow by the handle with their left hand. The grip should be loose and comfortable, with the **wrist straight in alignment** with the rest of the arm. If you are shooting a bow without a shelf or rest, the arrow shaft will sit atop the index finger knuckle of this hand.

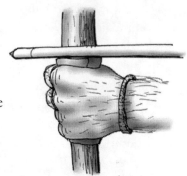

3. DRAW

While holding the bow and arrow with the grip described above, raise the bow to shoulder height. An archer's left arm should be straight, and the arrow already pointing in the general direction of the target. Now, with your right hand, pull the string and attached arrow back to your chin or face, whichever is your anchor point (more on that later). The draw should be smooth and unhurried. If an archer has to groan with exertion or point the arrow away from the target to draw, then they need a lighter bow.

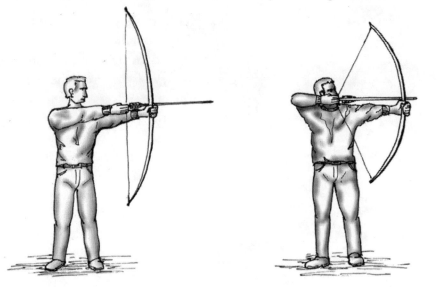

---

3. See the biography on Ishi for more on this. The technique is described by Saxton Pope in *Hunting with the Bow and Arrow* (p. 25)

An alternative method of drawing is the "push" method. Instead of keeping the bow arm straight, you start with it bent and your arrow already held at your anchor point. Then, you press the bow towards the target with your bow arm, out to full draw. This style was popular with several Native American tribes, as well as the famous archer Fred Bear. I don't interfere if students want to draw this way, but I don't teach it because I find it awkward. Whichever style of draw you use, be mindful to never release the string at full draw without an arrow on it; it could damage the bow, string, or both.

4. ANCHOR

To get consistent, precise shots it's important that the bow be held in exactly the same way each time. By having a memorized anchor point, an archer can assure consistency. There are several good anchor points, and each person will be comfortable with a different one— experiment! For me, I draw until the largest knuckle on my thumb touches the corner of my jaw, just below my ear. Archers with longer arms might draw until the 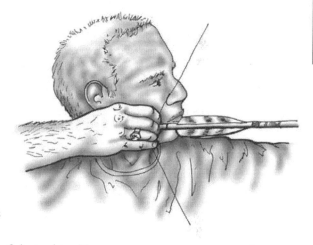 string touches the center of their chin. I've seen many variations, such as:

➥ Touching your thumb to your earlobe
➥ Sticking your thumb in your ear
➥ Touching your middle finger to your cheek
➥ Touching your middle finger to the corner of your mouth
➥ Using a kisser button that touches your lip

The important part is that once you decide on an anchor point, stick with it and perfect it.

TEACHING

5. AIM

There are several methods of aiming, and different ones are appropriate for different students. I'll explain each in depth, but first let's talk about which you should be teaching.

When teaching archery to young ones or total novices, the main goal is to get arrows moving in the general direction of the target without anyone getting hurt. Whether they know it or not, they will be building *instinctive aiming* experience with every shot. This is a good method for kids to learn, and it's easy to teach: just let them keep shooting until they get better.

However, what will eventually happen (especially with older kids) is they will expect to be shown the Ancient Secrets of Archery, at which time you will want to explain *gap shooting*. I prefer to teach it because it's an aiming system they can take home with them and have forever. And I believe in it, because it's the system I personally use and it's never let me down. I generally don't explain this system right off, though, because it can add a lot of confusion when they're first getting started.

Teaching kids to use a *mechanical sight* is not the norm, but might be appropriate in certain instances. Use your judgment. If you have all the equipment available and your students have their own bows so they don't have to adjust the sights every time, then go for it.

Other styles like *point-of-aim* are interesting to know about, but aren't really practical for most archery instruction. So, on with the explanations!

Instinctive aiming

Much like throwing a ball, through hours and hours of practice the archer's mind learns to instinctively calculate where the arrow will land. The archer simply concentrates on the target, and shoots. This is the original, no-frills way to aim a bow. [4] Instinctive aiming was described as early as 1545 by Roger Ascham, who disliked the other systems of aiming and said "...having a man's eye always on his mark is the only way to shoot straight."

Advantages:

+ You don't need any fancy equipment or sights.
+ It works in any lighting situation or weather.
+ It's fast.
+ It works at many different distances.

---

4.   Although it's been around since the beginning, this system was popularized by Howard Hill, one of the greatest archers of all time. Few could match his skill with the bow, which says a lot for this technique, but bear in mind that he shot over 150 arrows every day in practice his entire life. Likewise, in 1878 Maurice Thompson said, "There is no such thing as 'taking aim' with an arrow. He is a bungling archer who attempts it."

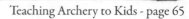

Disadvantages:
- It takes the most practice to get right.
- It is less accurate at distances you don't practice.

To practice *instinctive aiming*, develop a consistent stance and release. Concentrate on the target, keep both eyes open, and shoot a LOT of arrows until they automatically go where your mind wills them.

Gap shooting

This system that strikes a middle ground between instinctive aiming and mechanical sights. The archer uses a bare bow, like instinctive shooting, but estimates the correct aiming point by looking at the visual gap between the point of the arrow and the center of the target, essentially using the arrowhead as a makeshift sight.

Advantages:
+ You don't need any fancy equipment or sights.
+ It's fast.
+ It works at many different distances.
+ You get accurate results with less practice than instinctive shooting.

Disadvantages:
- It is less accurate at distances you don't practice.
- The archer must roughly know the distance to the target.
- It is thrown off by different arrowheads or longer/shorter arrows.

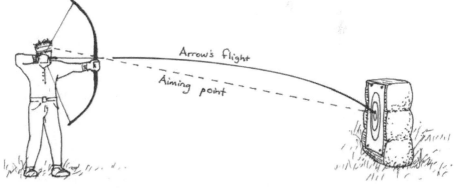

To practice *gap shooting*, you need to adjust your focus so you can see the arrowhead and the target at the same time. Place the arrowhead so it covers the center of the target, and release. If it lands in the center of the target, congratulations! You are at the distance called "point-blank range", or

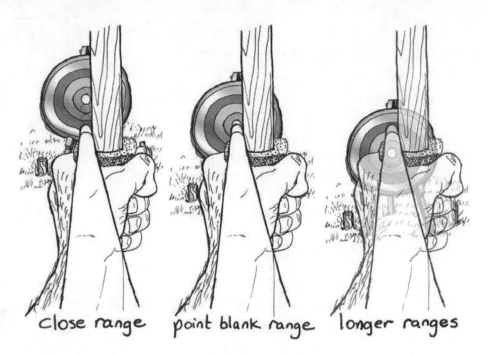

close range   point blank range   longer ranges

that distance where no vertical adjustment is needed for aiming. More likely than not, though, your arrow will land high or low. Load a second arrow, notice how many arrowhead diameters your first shot missed by, and then adjust your aim the same distance in the opposite direction. With practice, you will learn how much space (or *gap*) should be between the arrowhead and the target for a given distance. For a more thorough explanation of *gap shooting*, I recommend reading *Beginners Guide to Traditional Archery*, by Brian J. Sorrells.

Mechanical sights

These are devices attached to a bow to help in aiming. To use a mechanical sight, the archer simply places a dot, pin, or crosshair on the center of the intended target and releases. There are numerous types of sights available, but they all have a few things in common. First, for them to work properly, the archer must anchor their draw exactly the same way every time. To aid in this, some archers add kisser buttons or peep sights woven into the string. In addition, the archer must know the range to their target, so they can use the correct pin or adjust the sight accordingly. The sight then compensates for the amount of arrow drop at the given distance.

Advantages:

+ It's extremely accurate.

+ Once properly adjusted, much less practice is needed.

Disadvantages:
- Additional (sometimes costly) equipment required.
- The archer must know the distance to the target.
- In low-light situations, the pins can be hard to see.
- Sights need to be adjusted when new, any time they get dropped or bumped, and whenever anything else changes, such as arrow weight or archer.

To use a *mechanical sight*, you first must sight in. There are many kinds of sights, but they all work on the same basic principal as the pin sight. Stand at a measured distance from the target and select a pin for that range. Draw the bow and place the pin on the center of the target, and shoot. Then, draw a second arrow and aim in the same fashion. Note how far the first arrow is off the mark, both vertically and horizontally. Relax your draw, then adjust the sights in the same direction & distance that the first arrow missed by. Repeat this process several times, fine-tuning it until the arrow lands in the center of the target. For each different distance you want to shoot from, add an additional pin that is sighted in for that range.

Once your sights are adjusted, using them is quite simple. Draw the bow to your anchor point, and place the pin for the distance you're shooting right on the center of the target and release. Your arrow should land on target. As an interesting side note, you can improvise a makeshift pin sight by placing a strip of masking tape on the back of your bow, and slipping sewing pins under it at the correct locations.

TEACHING

Point-of-aim method

This ancient method is a close cousin to gap shooting, except the archer places a marker on the ground[5] or notes a distinctive rock or twig, then aims the arrowhead at it before releasing. It's a lot like gap shooting, but without visualizing the gap. It shares the same advantages as gap shooting, but has a few added disadvantages:

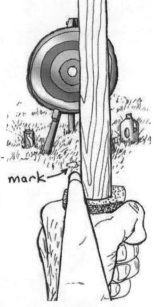

mark→

- It doesn't work at distances longer than point-blank range.

- It's really inconvenient when there is nothing on the ground to use for aiming.

In general, this isn't a very practical method to teach, and is not as effective as the other methods.

---

5.   Ascham frowned on this as cheating, mentioning an archer who was known to place his quiver on the ground between the shooting line and the target, to use as an aiming point. The archer claimed it was so he could watch his equipment to discourage thieves.

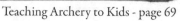

Sometimes it helps to have visual aids to assist your students. You can use a photocopier to enlarge the target and bow illustrations on these pages, and then glue them to cardboard and cut them out. By moving the picture of the bow and arrow over the target, you can show your students what different aiming pictures look like and how to correct for off-target shots.

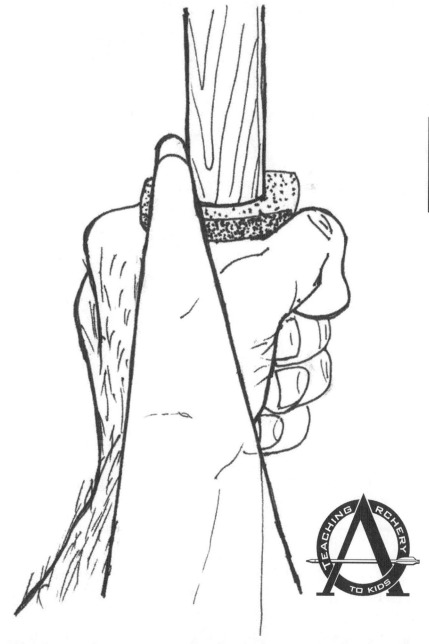

6. RELEASE

You've aimed, but you're not yet done. You still need to send the arrow on its way. Ideally, the release should be crisp and smooth, so as to not change the arrow's flight path. For a good release, gradually relax the muscles of your fingers, being careful not to let your anchor point move at all. When your fingers are relaxed enough, the string will suddenly leave your hand, almost as a surprise. It's simple, but there are several ways it can go wrong, so keep your eye out for:

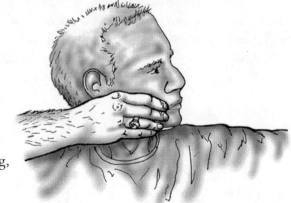

The Jerk: If the archer jerks their hand, the arrow will not go where it was pointed. After the shot, the hand should be right where it was before the shot. Sometimes I put my finger on the back of a students hand and hold it there while they aim, to make apparent to them how far their hand moves when they release.

The Push: Some beginners want to give the arrow a little more "oomph" by starting it on its way with a little push. Unfortunately, this has the opposite effect. No one can push an arrow as fast as a bowstring, so what ends up happening is the shot starts at wherever the pushing stops, as though the bow was only drawn part way. Again, the fix for this is to concentrate on not letting the anchor hand move during the release.

The Flinch: Bows are under a lot of tension, and all that built up energy can be scary, especially if the student's arm has been slapped by the string before, or worse, if they've had a string break on them. Work with the student until they have had several painless shots, and flinching will eventually go away.

The Wobble: It can be difficult to maintain a steady anchor if you are tired, have too heavy a bow, or are holding it too long. If you see a student struggling to hold the bow at full draw, get them a bow with less draw weight.

Also, with really young students, you occasionally see them let go of the arrow, but not the string. The arrow clatters to the ground, and they get a terrified/ befuddled expression as they are left holding the bow at full draw with no arrow. Avoid the temptation to laugh (though it IS pretty funny

looking!), then tell them to relax. When they try it again, encourage them to let go of the *string*, and not think about the arrow at all; it will go all by itself once the string is in motion.

7. FOLLOW THROUGH

The final step in every good shot, as in most sports, is follow through. Once your arrow is on the way to the target, hold your position and watch it go. Don't move anything until it's been in the target a second or two. Then, let your arms relax down to your sides, and prepare to load another arrow. There are several reasons for follow-through:

➺ It prevents you from accidentally moving too early, and messing up your shot.
➺ It allows you to check your body position to make sure it's correct.
➺ It gives you a chance to watch the arrow's flight, to notice any wiggling or other bad flight characteristics.
➺ It lets you see where your arrows are hitting, so your brain can subconsciously adjust your intuitive aiming mechanism.

Those are the seven simple steps to shooting archery. At first, you will want to make sure your students are doing every step distinctly, but after a while, some steps will happen very quickly and blend into other steps. Stance will become automatic, for example, and the draw will blend into the anchor. If you'd like to see the whole process in action, riffle the top right corner of this book to make a brief animation of an archer shooting an arrow.

Sample Lessons

Here are a few sample lessons. These are only examples of how I've done it in the past, to give you some ideas to start with when designing your own class. You will need to modify this model or invent one entirely your own, depending on your equipment, the number of archers you have, the size of your range, the amount of time for the class, and many other variables. As your experience with teaching archery grows, pay attention to what works and what doesn't, and modify your class accordingly. Don't be afraid to try new things, either: if you get into the habit of doing the exact same thing every time, you will get bored with teaching, and the lack of enthusiasm will transmit through to the kids.

TEACHING

Lesson #1 – Archery Introduction

OVERVIEW

If possible, it helps to have a chance to sit with your students before bows and arrows are within reach, to discuss some of the basics of what will happen. This brief introductory talk helps them feel less nervous about what is going on, as well as giving them time to absorb all the terminology and information before they have to use it. They will also listen better when they don't have bows and arrows to misguide their attention.

In this sample class, the archers are 24 kids at summer camp, aged 10 to 12, and are visiting the range briefly during a round-robin tour of the camp. I will chat briefly with them at the archery range for about half an hour, to give them an introduction to what Archery will be like. Only one bow and one arrow are available, for me to use as props during the discussion.

CLASS PREPARATION

➡ Clean the range.
➡ Make sure posters of bow and arrow parts are visible.
➡ Have one bow and one arrow available for demonstration.
➡ Have bracers nearby but out of sight.

GOALS

➡ Students should be able to name the parts of the bow and arrow.
➡ Students should know how to behave at the range, and generally what to expect when they arrive in the future.

CLASS OUTLINE

Introduce myself, and ask the names of the kids. Although I often can't remember all the names, just knowing one or two can really help get them to open up.

Ask them how much they know about archery. Sometimes, if a kid is particularly knowledgeable, you can get them to answer questions you pose, further engaging the class.

Stress safety.

Explain the rules of the range. Give examples where it helps eliminate confusion.

Explain the parts of the bow and arrows. I find the most effective way to do this is by making a game out of it, where I point to a part and say its

name, then have them repeat it back to me. Afterwards, you can test them by pointing to a part and asking them to name it. When they know the names of the parts, it makes teaching them to shoot a little easier.

If time permits, let them try putting on the bracers.

Children more easily and sooner may be taught to shoot excellently than men, because children may be taught to shoot well at the first, men have more to unlearn their ill uses.
-Roger Ascham, 1545

TEACHING

Lesson #2 ~ Learning to Shoot

OVERVIEW

Here's an example of how I conduct a beginning archery class. This is the same group of students as before: 24 kids at summer camp, aged 10 to 12. They will be with me for an hour and a half and be returning to the archery range at least one more time before they are sent home for the summer. Two other adult leaders will be present to assist me during the class. I have seen this group before, and explained the basic information described in Lesson #1.

Some institutions, such as accredited summer camps, set a maximum ratio of archers to instructors. This number usually varies by age; check with your administrators. A good rule of thumb is that it is difficult to monitor and help more than about eight archers at once. If you have a class larger than this, you should break it down into rotations, where one group is shooting and another is watching and learning. After each end of six arrows, they switch. If you have a group larger than 16 archers, the students who are watching will have to sit for a long time— a disaster with younger kids. This is where additional help is critical. Non-instructing assistants can play games with the waiting kids, or read archery lore to them, or any number of other things as long as it doesn't distract the shooters from their task.

CLASS PREPARATION
- At the shooting line, set up eight shooting stations, each with a bow and six arrows.
- In the waiting area, set out a bin full of bracers.
- Have a bow and arrow in hand for demonstration.

GOALS
- Students should be able to successfully loose an arrow in the general direction of the target.
- Students should exhibit safe archery practices.

CLASS OUTLINE

Test archers on the various parts of the bow and arrow, as well as safety rules. If they have much trouble recalling the previous lesson, I spend a little time reviewing.

While the students are sitting in the waiting area, I demonstrate the proper place to stand on the shooting line, with one foot on either side of the line, shoulder width apart. Archers will face towards the right side of the field, one per station, close enough to the ground quivers to reach the arrows

without taking a step. Explain that any left handed archers should face the opposite direction, taking positions to the right of the range (as you face the targets), so they can see the instructor and other shooters.

Ask the first eight archers to take positions as I just demonstrated, **without touching any equipment** until instructed to do so. At this point, I usually move about 10 yards downrange so I can be clearly seen by all the archers. This is the one time it's OK to have someone downrange when there are arrows in the quivers, because as the instructor, I am facing the students and able to watch each one to make sure that they aren't nocking an arrow.

Once all are in the correct position, they may pick up a bow with their left hand, by the handle, with the shelf facing up and the string against the inside of their arm. Wait for them to figure this out, and help where needed; with younger archers, at least one bow will be upside down, backwards, or held in the wrong hand. Now is a good time to tell any left-handers that every time they hear me say "right", they should imagine I said "left", and vice-versa.

DEMONSTRATION

Now I will show them how to nock and shoot the arrow, but first I stress that **no one is allowed to touch any arrows yet**. In full view of the archers, I talk my way through the whole process, as I do it:

➡ With my right hand, I grab my arrow just in front of the fletching, and I reach across my chest to place the shaft atop the shelf.

➡ I rotate the arrow in my fingers, so the index feather is facing me (I ignore this step for really young kids, as it's confusing and doesn't make much difference at that skill level)

➡ I push the nock onto the string, just BELOW the nocking point, ans set the shaft on the shelf (or rest).

➡ I hold the three shooting fingers of my right hand aloft, explaining that these are the only ones you touch the string with. One finger goes above the arrow, and two below. The string should touch the fingers between the first joint and the tip of the fingers.

➡ I place my fingers on the string, demonstrating the one-over, two-under position and how my hand is open, not closed in a fist.

➡ I draw the arrow. To make it easier for them to see what is going on, I stand with my toes pointing towards the students, and aim to the side of the range. Obviously, you won't want to do this if it poses any danger to those outside the range.

The final part of the demonstration is shooting. I walk over and take a place straddling the shooting line, where all the students can see me. Then I shoot one arrow, repeating aloud the steps we just discussed.

The shot completed, I move to behind the shooting line, where I will stay for the rest of the lesson. The archers can now nock an arrow, but not yet fire. I verbally walk them through the nocking procedure I previously demonstrated, to help them remember. I check each archer, looking for arrows on the wrong side of the bow, nocks above the nocking point, and on older students, the index feather facing the wrong way. If everyone is successful, we go on to...

THEIR FIRST SHOT

I allow each archer to take their first shot one at a time, with me to watch over their shoulder. I correct any major mistakes that might affect safety, but otherwise it's best to let them do what they will, as they are processing a lot of new information right now.

If each archer has completed their first shot without endangering themselves or anyone else, then tell them they can shoot the rest of their arrows in their own time. When they are done, they are to set their bow down and wait patiently at the shooting line for my next instructions.

Once all the arrows have been shot and all the bows have been set down, then I step back onto the range to explain and demonstrate the arrow retrieval procedure:

I remind them that running is not allowed.

Arrows that went behind the targets are collected first. This is a good habit to get into, because you or a student might one day want to use an uncontrolled range. If you leave the arrows in the target and collect them last, then it will be apparent to anyone who comes along that there is someone in the bushes looking for arrows, and it would be a bad idea to just start shooting.

Once all the arrows behind the target are collected, we walk up to the targets. Any arrows on the ground are picked up immediately, even if they belong to other archers. We never step over them, otherwise they might get stepped on (and broken).

I demonstrate arrow removal, with one hand on the face to keep it from tearing, and being mindful of anyone standing in front of the target so as avoid poking them with the nock end of the arrow. If you are working with older kids or a more experienced group, then this would be an appropriate time to explain the scoring system.

Everyone can now pull their arrows, and return them to the ground quivers. If anyone does not have six arrows, then I stop and help them resolve the problem.

By this point, the group of archers that just shot can go sit in the ready area, and the next group can take positions on the line. Then, I go back to the first step of the demonstration and repeat it for the new group.

If this all seems extremely structured and parochial, it is. Young archers with no idea what is going on will feel more confident in this sort of ordered environment, and it makes it easier for the instructor to keep an eye on safety. But, this doesn't mean that classes have to stay this way for long. As a group of students gains experience and can demonstrate they have the maturity to help be responsible for their own safety, you can gradually relax the format of the shooting, such as in the next lesson.

TEACHING

illustration by Frank Victoria

Lesson #3 – More Advanced Archers

OVERVIEW
In this class, the kids are a little older, maybe 14 years old. They've shot with me several times, and are quite familiar with the range, rules, and skills. There are eight archers in this group.

CLASS PREPARATION
➤ At the shooting line, set up eight shooting stations, each with a bow and six arrows.
➤ In the waiting area, set out a bin full of bracers.
➤ Tack up specialty targets on the butts.

GOALS
➤ Students should have an enjoyable time shooting.
➤ Students should get time to practice their skills, fostering improvement.
➤ Students should exhibit safe archery practices.

CLASS OUTLINE
Test archers on the various parts of the bow and arrow, and safety rules. If they have much trouble recalling the previous lesson, I spend a little time reviewing.

Explain the game or specialty shoot of the day. Demonstrate, if necessary.

Allow the archers to proceed at their own pace. When they are done, they should set their bow down and wait for everyone else to finish.

Walk from archer to archer as they are shooting, answering questions and giving pointers to help with technique. I try not to give too much advice to any single person on a given day, or else they just get overloaded and don't remember anything.

When all the archers are done and the bows are on the ground, walk back with the archers to collect arrows. Occasionally, advice can be given to students based on where and how the arrows landed in the targets.

Teaching Tips & Ideas

Once you've taught a few lessons, you will start to notice some problems that are commonplace, as well as some that are more specific and require special attention or knowledge to fix. Let's look at some of these, and ideas on how to solve them.

THE THREE BIG FORM PROBLEMS

Much of your instructing after the first lesson will involve just watching archers shoot, and pointing out ways they can improve their form. There are a lot of subtle things that go into good form, but there are three things that you will say to your students over and over:

1) Elbow up

The elbow of your drawing arm should be at about the same height as your hands, maybe even a little higher. This position engages all of your back and shoulder muscles, making it easier to draw and hold for aiming. It also forces your hand to be closer to your face, making your anchor point more precise.

2) Stand tall

When shooting, the correct posture is very similar to when you're just standing around, talking to your pals or watching the scenery. You don't need to bend forward, backwards, left, or right at the hips; you should be comfortable, balanced, and straight. Be a proud archer! You're learning an ancient and noble art.

3) Pull all the way back

Figure your anchor point, and draw all the way to it every time. Failure to do so gives you erratic and underpowered shots. This is the most common problem with young archers, for a combination of reasons. They sometimes worry that the bow will snap, so they're scared to pull "hard". Show them how far to pull it, and let them get comfortable with that amount of force needed. For others, they simply don't have the strength to pull it all the way. Get them a lighter bow immediately; they're using the wrong one. In some cases, students just forget about the anchor point entirely. Keep reminding them, and soon it will become natural for them.

STRING SLAP AND SHOULDER ROLL

As I've mentioned several times before, a serious problem to watch for is string slap. It's painful, and can put people off of archery permanently if they're not taught how to avoid it. Proper form is the key. A common place for new archers to be struck with the string is just inside the left elbow. This comes from allowing their left arm to relax during the draw, locking the elbow. The locked elbow actually bends a little bit the wrong way, pushing it into the path of the string. In general, young girls have the most trouble with this, for two reasons: oftentimes they have less muscle available to hold their arm straight, so they let their joint do the work instead. Their extreme flexibility also allows their elbow to move farther inward than the less-flexible boys or adults. But anyone shooting with a locked elbow should try to avoid it, because it puts more strain on your joint than allowing your muscles to do the work they were intended for.

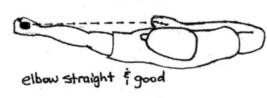

elbow straight & good

↓ elbow too far out

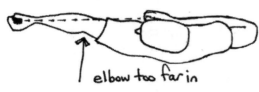

↑ elbow too far in

Fixing the problem is relatively straightforward, once you identify it. First, make sure your students use their arm muscles, making a conscious effort to hold their elbows in a straight position. Then, teach the archers to roll their shoulders slightly forward. This further engages the triceps, while

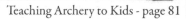

also moving the bottom of the elbow farther away from the string's path.

ARROW WANDERING OFF OF THE REST

Occasionally with new archers, they have a problem with the arrow drifting off of the rest while they're aiming. This is usually because they are pinching the arrow nock between their fingers, and the pressure is gently pushing the arrow off the rest. The solution is to spread their drawing fingers far enough apart so they only touch the bowstring, not the arrow itself. It's rare, but sometimes the arrow wanders off of the rest because the nock fits tightly to the string, and the student is actually rolling the string because of a peculiar draw. Teach them to make sure their hand is open when they draw, with only the very tips of the fingers curved around the string, not balled into a fist around the string. As a last resort, if these other techniques fail, have them grab the string at the first joint of their fingers, rather than the pad, and roll the string out to the center of their finger pads right before they draw.

A related issue is bow angle. When you are drawing, it's OK to lean your bow over a little to help the arrow stay on the rest, but when you shoot, the bow should be perpendicular to the horizon. If it's not straight up-and-down, then your aiming will be slightly off, and the error will become quite noticeable when you start shooting at longer distances. Encourage your students to always hold the bow straight, so they don't develop bad habits that will haunt them later.

TEACHING

GETTING TANGLED UP

The scenario: your very young archer wants to get the arrow nocked, but doesn't have enough hands to hold the string, the bow, the arrow, their lollipop, a toad, and every thing else at the same time. What's a kid to do? First, they stick the bow between their knees. Then, they grab the bow with their right hand, and try to switch the arrow to their left. Pretty soon, it's a big tangled mess. The solution? Tell them that their left hand should hold the handle of the bow, and never leave it under any circumstance, as if it were glued there with superglue. Everything else that needs to be done in archery can be done with just the right hand, and a little patience.

LEFT- AND RIGHT- HANDEDNESS

Occasionally with younger kids, you will get some that do not know if they are left-handed or right-handed. There are two ways to handle this. You could simply assume they are right handed and teach them that way. If they are actually left-handed but they've never shot before, then it won't be any more difficult than learning left-handed, and will make it easier for them to get equipment when they are older.

The other option is to "discover" their handedness. Casually hand them an arrow, and pay silent attention to which hand they grab it with. That is a pretty accurate indicator of handedness.

Some coaches believe that regardless of your handedness, you should draw the arrow with the hand that's on the same side as your dominant eye. We'll talk more on eye dominance in a bit.

As an interesting side note, there was once a lot of prejudice against the left-handed, both in the archery world and society in general. In the late 19th century, tournament rule #18 of the *Wabash Merry Archers* stated that "no archer shall be allowed on the grounds if he is known to shoot left-handed."

EYE DOMINANCE

Most people have a *dominant eye*, or one they naturally use more than the other. In most of life, this is unnoticeable, but in archery, it can be a problem because you can only look down the arrow with one eye at a time. The ideal situation is if your dominant eye is the one that already looks down the arrow (the right eye, in right-handed archers). If you're not so fortunate, then you're in the cross-dominant crowd like me; that is, you are right handed and left eye dominant (or the reverse). When you aim you might get dizzy, or see the arrow misaligned with the target, or have some other weird optical illusion.

If you suspect a student is having trouble with eye dominance issues, there are a few easy ways to tell which of their eyes is dominant. One way is

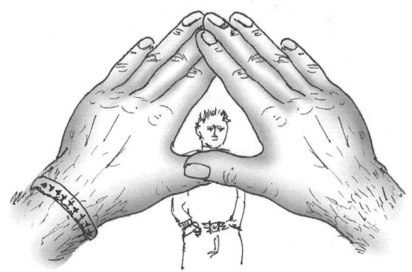

to have them hold an arrow at arm's length, and point it at something. You can look backwards along the arrow, and see which eye it points to. Another more dramatic way is to have them look you in the eye from about 10 feet away, then bring their arms together between your face and theirs, making a small hole between their hands as shown in the picture to the right. Now, ask them to slowly move their hands back to their face, keeping your eye centered in the hole. They will bring the hole right up to their dominant eye.

To help cross-dominant archers, there are two options. The first is to close your left (non-aiming) eye when shooting. This is not ideal, because having both eyes open gives you depth perception, allowing you to properly judge the distance to the target.

The second option is to shoot left-handed. One school of thought suggests that all archers be taught left- or right-handed shooting based on their eye dominance. This could be a problem for right-handed archers with a dominant left eye if they've shot before, and are accustomed to shooting right handed. It could also doom them to a life of having to find left-handed equipment. Usually, it makes more sense to just have them close their dominant eye.

TEACHING

PRECISION VS. ACCURACY

precise

accurate (and not)

precise & accurate

In beginning archery instruction, the goal we are working towards is precision. Accuracy is a secondary concern, because it can be achieved easily after archers have good precision. So what is the difference?

Precision is the ability to put arrows consistently in the same place. *Accuracy* is the ability to put an arrow where you want it. You might think that accuracy is the goal of archery, but it really isn't.

Suzy the Archer puts two arrows over the backstop, two in the outer rings, and two in the bullseye, to the cheers of her classmates. Those last two arrows were very *accurate*, and she should be congratulated for her good shooting, but the inconsistency of her shooting means that she has a lot more to learn than her neighbor, Alecia. At 30 yards, Alecia grouped all her arrows within eight inches of each other. Even though they were at the bottom left of the target, she has *precision*, and that means her shooting can be easily improved. She just needs to adjust her aim an equal amount in the opposite direction, and will be beating the socks off of everyone else with just a little more practice.

TALL ARCHERS AND DRAW-THROUGH

When teaching kids, the equipment is often sized for people with pretty short arms. There is a danger with tall kids and short arrows that they will "draw through", bringing the point past the inside belly of the bow. This is a dangerous situation, because if the archer releases in this condition, the arrow can get crushed between the bow and string, sending flying shards of shaft in every direction (including into your student's forearm). The only real way to guarantee it won't happen is to have some longer arrows on hand for tall archers to use.

Teaching Archery

DISTANCE

Start with big targets at short distances, then increase the distances as your students improve. Maurice Thompson said it best in 1878:

> *Always use a four-foot target even if you begin shooting at ten yards. Nothing so much assists the progress of good shooting as for every arrow to keep within the circumference of the target; the archer can then note exactly the effect of each shot, and by comparison measure his constant advance in skill.*

WHISTLES

Many archery instruction texts advocate the use of a whistle, to let archers know when to move to the line, when to shoot, and when it's clear to retrieve arrows. I am against the use of whistles, for several reasons:

➻ I despise having a whistle blown at me, so I don't inflict it on my students.

➻ A whistle is just a noise; it doesn't actually tell the archers what to do unless you invent some sort of code, based on the number of blasts. A code is just another thing young archers could forget, and could lead to confusion or a dangerous misunderstanding. It would be a disaster if someone thought two blasts meant "retrieve arrows", when it actually meant "start shooting".

➻ The extreme volume of a whistle is unnecessary in most teaching environments. A loudly spoken command such as "archers, you may fire" can be heard clearly, and is unmistakable in its meaning.

➻ Should something dangerous suddenly occur at the range, most instructors will get a big adrenaline rush, making it easy to yell "STOP!" as loud as a whistle anyway.

TEACHING

In my school-days,
  when I had lost one shaft,
I shot his fellow
  of the selfsame flight
The selfsame way
  with more advised watch
To find the other forth,
  and by adventuring both
I oft found both.

~William Shakespeare
The Merchant of Venice

What kind of fun stuff can you do with bows and arrows? Your imagination is the limit. This chapter has a list of ideas, generally organized from easiest to most difficult. Some of the games at the end of this chapter aren't practical for programs without elaborate facilities, but they are presented so you can have a thorough overview of the varied types of games that can be played with archery.

When you're picking activities, it will be more enjoyable for your students if you pick ones that are challenging enough to keep them interested, but not so hard that they get discouraged. And, as with all archery, you need to constantly evaluate the safety with which the activity is being carried out. Now...

Let the games begin!

TARGET ARCHERY

This is archery at its most basic: shooting a set number of arrows from a fixed distance at target faces with concentric circles. It's the mainstay of beginning practice, and helps build consistency. But it doesn't have to be boring, and you can constantly change the variables. Try shooting from longer or shorter distances, at larger or smaller targets, and so forth.

I generally use a 48" or 32" target face because it's easier for the younger ones to hit at short range, and I score by color: 5 points for gold, 4 for red, 3 for blue, 2 for black, and 1 for white. Target archery tradition has it that any shot that breaks the line between colors counts as the higher value, and arrows that bounce out of the target are worth nothing. With this system, the maximum score on a six-arrow end is 30. You can award prizes for high scores (say, 25 and above) or keep a "board of honor" with the names of high-scoring archers. These sort of motivational devices can be a lot of fun, as long as the students don't get too obsessive about it.

There's a wide variety of "official" rounds, as well. They consist of several *ends*, or groups of arrows shot and retrieved from different distances. You can get the official description of many of these rounds online or from national (and international) archery organizations, but I will give you the FITA round as an example:

ACTIVITIES

Target Face Diameter	Number of Arrows	Men's Distance	Women's Distance	Junior Distance	Cadet Distance
122 cm (48")	6 ends of 6	90 m	70 m	50 m	35 m
122 cm (48")	6 ends of 6	70 m	60 m	40 m	25 m
80 cm (32")	6 ends of 6	50 m	50 m	30 m	20 m
80 cm (32")	6 ends of 6	30 m	30 m	20 m	10 m

That's a total of 144 arrows, quite a lot of shooting! Scoring is based on a standard target face, with 10 points for the inner gold, 9 for outer gold, 8 for inner red, 7 for outer red, and so on down to 1 point for outer white. I've included target face diagrams in the Crafts section, if you want to give this a try.

TOURNAMENTS

Tournaments can be as basic, or elaborate, as you want. A simple tournament might involve each archer shooting six arrows at 20 yards, adding up each archer's score, and declaring the highest scoring archer the victor.

If theatrics is more your style, then make a pageant out of the tournament. Build up anticipation days in advance by talking up the event, encouraging practice, and so forth. Make prizes known beforehand as well; an excellent mini-arrow trophy can be made from a broken arrow refitted with a new head, painted gold and lettered with the date and name of the tournament. When the day of the tournament arrives, announce the names of each archer, and have a multi-round elimination system, where six or more archers shoot at once, with the two best advancing to the next round. Depending on your total number of students and their enthusiasm for this sort of thing, it could turn into a fun, hours-long event.

For students who will be around for a while, a multi-day tournament with additive scores might be more appropriate. At the end of each class, have the archers shoot their "tournament round". Count their score, and add it to the running total. Make a poster with a graph showing their progress over time, and after a predetermined number of days, end the tournament and award prizes to the highest scorers.

MONSTER SHOOT

It can be fun and a change of pace to draw "monsters" on the target faces. This might also be appropriate for certain times of the year, like Halloween. You should use a little judgment, though, and weigh the local social and political climate before you give this a try; for some groups, this might be inappropriate. And if you are having the kids paint their own target faces, keep an eye on them as they work, looking out for recognizable figures, classmates, etc. If any of that starts, try to steer them away from it or just change the game entirely to one of the many others that are available.

CALLED SHOTS

This is a variant of target shooting, where the archers wait and shoot one arrow at a time, at targets you call out. This game can be mixed with others such as balloon shooting, but is a lot of fun with the standard target face as well. If your range has an adequate safe area behind and to the sides, it is even possible to have archers shoot at each other's targets. This is a little disconcerting at first, but they will like it once the idea sets in, and it's good practice for estimating distances other than the standard ones. A typical call might be "everyone shoot an arrow at the second target from the right."

TIC-TAC-TOE AND BOARDGAMES

You can make target-sized gameboards with butcher paper and tempera paint. Pin them to the target butts, and you're ready to play, using arrows as game pieces. Tic-Tac-Toe and Othello are good games for this. Two archers share the same game board, and take turns shooting at squares they want. An arrow captures whatever square it lands in, unless there's already an arrow there. Misses sometimes give amusing results! It helps for each archer to have arrows with different fletchings.

DARTCHERY

This is special archery board game that follows the rules for Darts, and is played as such except you shoot arrows instead of throwing darts. It requires a special target face that has the same markings as a dart board; you can make these with a compass, protractor, and tempera paint (see the Crafts section for more information).

BALLOONS, CANS, AND FRUITS

Who can resist things that go POP? Inflate a lot of balloons, and tape them to the target butts for the students to shoot at. Anything that is relatively soft can be used as a 3-D target as well, such as soda cans, apples, and paper cups. Place these objects on top of a cardboard box a few feet in front of the target butt. Award 5 points for piercing the item, 3 for knocking it off, and 1 for touching it. For a grand finale, bring out a watermelon, and let everyone shoot at it at the same time. When the round is over, retrieve it and cut it up for everyone to eat (this was the all-time favorite activity at my camp).

WAND SHOOT

Medieval archers in centuries past would challenge themselves with a *wand shoot.* In this ancient form of target practice, a thin willow wand measuring two inches wide by six feet high was stuck in the ground, and archers tried to hit it from 100 yards away. Obviously, this will be impossible for all but the most skilled archers, but you can make a fun version of the wand shoot by placing the wand a few inches in front of the normal target butt, or simply placing a stripe of duct tape vertically in the

center of the target face. Assign 5 points for a direct hit on the wand, and 2 for touching it.

This activity is a good exercise for intermediate archers, because it lets them focus on the left-right portion of aiming, ignoring the vertical variances introduced by range and inconsistent draw length.

CHEROKEE CORNSTALK SHOOT

This traditional Cherokee archery contest is in some ways similar to the *wand shoot*, but its goal is entirely different. Instead of trying to hit a single wand, you are trying to hit a giant rack of cornstalks three feet wide, three feet high, and a foot thick. The challenge is to see how many cornstalks you can pierce. It is a test of strength, as heavier draw weight bows will push an arrow through more stalks. But it is also a test of accuracy and technique, because you need to be able to hit the rack to score, and an arrow that doesn't have a straight flight path will not pierce the stalks as effectively. Traditionally, this contest is shot from 80 yards, and a point is awarded for each stalk pierced. Archers take turns shooting, with the first archer reaching 50 points declared the winner[1].

You can play a scaled-down version of this with your students, using your standard range and backstop. Collect wrapping paper spindles or other cardboard tubes, or make tubes from rolled butcher paper or newsprint. Bundle them together, and pin them to your target butts. Special arrowheads are used for the actual Cherokee Cornstalk Shoot, but regular field or target points will work fine for these softer materials. Some experimentation will help you to find what materials will allow your lighter bows to penetrate properly.

FIELD ARCHERY

All of the previously described games are variations of target archery. Field archery is different, in that the archer shoots from many different locations. Archery ranges with field courses are common; a quick search in the phone book or online might turn up one near you. These field courses are set up much like golf courses, sprawling through the woods and hills. At the first station, you shoot one (or several) arrows at the target downrange. Then, once all shooters have finished, the group moves downrange to collect arrows. From there, the next target is visible, and you shoot at it from where you stand (or a designated shooting box). You proceed through the course this way, moving from target to target, in a merry voyage across the landscape.

Some ranges have markers telling you the range to the targets, and some have special shooting stations for women or children. Targets placed between trees, across ravines, or at long distances are common. Field archery is extremely exciting and challenging, even for experienced archers.

As an instructor, you need to pay extra attention when running a field archery course. Keep your archers close together, and be watchful of where they are pointing their arrows. Field archery is one of the few situations where young archers will be walking around with bow and arrows in hand, so teach them proper care when carrying them. For really younger archers, I usually only allow them one arrow each. When they miss the target, they will pay closer attention to where the arrow went if it's their only one. But more importantly, it makes it easier to know at a glance who has and hasn't

1.   Information courtesy of the Cherokee Nation. Learn more at www.cherokee.org .

shot yet. If you do this, make sure you take extra arrows and carry them with you, in case someone breaks theirs or legitimately loses it.

It's always a good idea to leave your arrows in the target while you are looking for those you've lost in the woods, but in field archery, this is life-threateningly important. Since you often can't see archers a few targets behind or ahead of you, these arrows left in the target, along with your bow leaning against the target face, are the best ways to let archers following you know that it's not yet safe to start shooting. Another point of etiquette for field archery is that if you find someone else's arrow, stick it in the top of the target butt so it's highly visible. Some ranges even have "found arrow" bins; if so, use them.

What can you do if there isn't a field archery course near you? Well, you can always set up your own, if you are inventive and sensible. If you have woods or fields that can be made off-limits during the times you wish to shoot, you can lay out a course where archers move from target to target, shooting as they go. If you do this, be certain that every target has an appropriate safe area behind it and to the sides. Most established field archery courses have been carefully designed to allow multiple parties to safely use the course simultaneously, but for a homemade course, do not allow more than one group to use it at the same time.

STUMP SHOOTING & KICKTARGETS

Stump shooting is an informal variant of field archery, and is great for its spontaneity and flexibility. When stump shooting, a small group of archers moves through woods and fields with their bows and arrows. The first shooter picks a target, such as a stump or mound of dirt, and announces it to the other archers. The size and range of the target can vary widely with the skill and mood of the archer, but it must have a safe area behind and to the sides, and not be ruined when it's full of arrow holes. Then, the lead archer shoots it, with each following shooter trying to hit the same mark. When the lead archer misses, a new archer takes over the job of lead archer. Though this kind of archery is a lot of fun, it's sometimes hard on arrows. The best arrow choices for stump shooting are blunts, Judo points, or field points mounted to a flexible, shock-resistant shaft such as cedar or fiberglass.

When your field doesn't really have any good natural targets, a *kick target* can be handy. They are available commercially, or you can make one yourself from a box or burlap sack stuffed with rags, or a big cube of high-density foam. The lead archer kicks or throws the target, and the entire group must shoot at it wherever it rests (the same safety rules apply, of course).

ARCHERY GOLF

Howard Hill wrote the first set of Archery Golf rules in 1928. In this game, archers play golf, using arrows instead of golf balls, and a bow instead of clubs. The "hole" is a tennis ball suspended on a wire hoop 4" above the ground.

Obviously, it's critical to get permission from the golf course before you do this (even though arrows damage the course less then club divots). The golf rule of "farthest out goes next" is followed, and no one ever gets closer to the hole than the shooter. This makes it possible to play mixed teams of golfers and archers; if you do so, the archers should start with a +18 stroke penalty[2] to make it fair.

CLOUT SHOOT

The clout shoot is another medieval archery game, intended to train soldiers to shoot extreme distances, into castles, and over obstacles. Instead of shooting a low-trajectory shot straight at the target, the archer shoots a high-trajectory shot "up and over". Obviously, a special range is required for this, as well as careful supervision. But it is not beyond the capability of a determined and resourceful instructor.

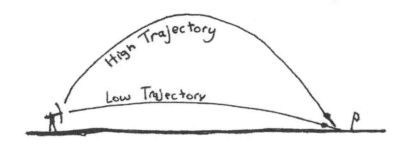

2. Thanks to the Centenary Archers Club (Queensland, Australia) for portions of this information.

The clout shoot is organized like target archery, except you are shooting at very long ranges and a very large target. To set up a clout range, you need a gigantic field clear of people, buildings, or anything breakable. *Clout* is an old English word for "cloth", which makes sense, as you are shooting at a brightly colored 12" square flag mounted to a short pole driven into the earth. Archers shoot from a firing line located far from the target, aiming their arrows so they fall into the earth as near to the flag as possible. Once all of the archers have shot, the arrows are scored with a pre-measured, multicolored rope with a loop around the clout pole. As the rope is walked around the pole, it traces a giant target on the ground, and arrows are given a score based on what color they touch on the rope (and therefore, how close they came to the pole). The scoring rope measurements[3] are as follows, from the loop outward:

Points	Color	GNAS length	FITA length
5	Gold	18 inches	3 meters
4	Red	18 inches	3 meters
3	Blue	3 feet	3 meters
2	Black	3 feet	3 meters
1	White	3 feet	3 meters
Overall		12 feet	15 meters

The distance and size of the target can be changed for lighter bows, but bear in mind that any bow can shoot quite far at full elevation, so plan your clear safety areas so that they are at least large enough that a stray arrow can't possibly leave the field.

If you have the space and ambition to try the "official" clout round, there are a few different versions, but each has six ends of six arrows (36 total) at these ranges:

---

3. GNAS is The Grand National Archery Society (Stropshire, England). Interestingly, they don't allow high trajectory shooting except for longbows.

180 yards/ 165 m	Men
140 yards/ 125 m	Women, boys under 18
120 yards/ 110 m	Girls under 18, boys under 16
100 yards/ 90 m	Girls under 16, boys under 14
80 yards/ 70 m	Girls under 13, boys under 12

Though they are both shot at the same distances, the FITA clout target is much larger than the GNAS clout target (30 meters in diameter, versus about 8 meters for the GNAS round). Whatever. The important part is to have fun!

FLIGHT ARCHERY

Simply put, flight archery is a competition to see who can shoot the farthest. It's not really well suited to an archery teaching program, but we'll talk about it a little anyway, for the sake of knowledge.

Flight archery courses have to be quite large. The ancient Turkish archers of the 1700s specialized in this sport, and regularly attained distances over 800 yards. The current record for a hand-pulled bow is 1,336 yards![4] In addition, competitive flight archers use a wide range of specialized, often handmade, equipment. Their arrows are shorter (16" long!), and their bows are highly modified. The official tournament rules for flight shooting aren't very consistent from country to country, either: in the USA, it is always done with the wind, and only six arrows are shot. In the UK, they shoot more arrows, but must overcome whatever wind is present at the field. In either case, an observer is allowed to give advice to the shooter; this is important, because the angle the shooter makes with the horizon is critical to getting the most distance out of the shot.

AERIAL TARGETS

Shooting at flying targets is an exciting way to challenge even the best archers. Howard Hill, arguably the greatest archer of all time, loved to demonstrate his aerial archery skill to the amazement of his spectators, and

---

4.   By Don Brown in 1987 (per FITA records)

this activity should be reserved for very advanced students. Throwable 12" foam disks specially designed for aerial archery are available from archery retailers, but a Frisbee tossed sideways can be just as effective in a pinch.

If you decide to try aerial archery, always use flu-flu arrows and ensure that you have an adequate safe area in any direction you could possibly shoot. BE EXTREMELY CAREFUL with where your bow is aimed at all times... if an archer is concentrating on the target, it increases that chance that their aim might drift across a bystander. It's a good idea to have several dedicated safety watchers in addition to the instructor, and never allow more than one shooter at a time. You will also have to be especially careful about the thrower. A thrower should never be ahead of the shooting line and should practice throwing well out into the archery range. Everyone should be well-trained to not shoot if there is a bad throw.

POPINJAY

Another medieval archery game, Popinjay is still popular in parts of France and Belgium. A tall pole is erected, up to 85 feet high, with wooden perches poking out like the branches of a tree. Upon these perches rest tiny artificial birds made from wood and feathers, the largest of which is the Popinjay that perches atop the main pole. Smaller targets ("hens" and "chicks") sit on lower branches. 5 points are scored

for the popinjay, 3 for a hen, and 1 for a chick. When the popinjay is unseated, the entire group is reset.

Like with other aerial shooting, great care must be taken to prevent the shooter and bystanders from being injured by falling arrows. Flu-flu arrows are used, with blunt points to dislodge the targets without damaging them.

ROVING MARK

Roving Mark, also known as *artillery shooting*, is an ancient English archery game that is a holdover from training medieval soldiers, and has been practiced since the late 1400s. It combines elements of field archery, stump shooting, and clout shooting. As in field archery, it uses a predetermined course with targets set up all over the hills and valleys of a country estate, at varying ranges from 80 to 280 yards. The archers proceed in a group from target to target, shooting three arrows at each target and scoring the closest.

Like stump shooting, the archers have to shoot at a wide variety of locations and unmarked ranges. In some cases, archers even shoot at very high angles to go over trees and obstacles. For tournaments, distance measuring equipment and bow sights are prohibited.

Roving Mark is most like the clout shoot, for several reasons. Due to the long ranges involved, most of the shots are high trajectory, with the arrows falling into the earth around the target. The target is a flagged pole, and scoring based on the distance from the pole. The Fraternity of St. George, an English archery society, scores arrows at half a bowlength from the target as 12 points, those within ¾ bowlength as 7 points, and those within the last quarter of the bow as 3 points. Since this game is traditionally shot with a longbow, these rather rough distances are based on a six-foot bow, making the entire target only 12 feet in diameter.

If this all sounds a little bit like golf with its random yardages, wandering course, and beautiful scenery, you might be interested to know that golf is a direct descendant of this game.

BEURSAULT

Whereas Roving Mark and Clout are popular in England, France has its own favorite medieval archery shoot, *Beursault*. The ranges were originally narrow, tree-lined paths 57 yards long and 4 yards wide[5], with a small structure standing at the end of the path containing a specially-sized target. In later times, entire gardens were built with multiple Beursault ranges, and the trees were sometimes replaced with spaced wooden panels. This allowed several archers on adjacent ranges to shoot and retrieve arrows simultaneously without endangering each other.

If you'd like to try shooting at the Beursault target face, there is a description of its measurements, coloration, and scoring in the Crafts section.

ACTIVITIES

---

5.   Thanks to www.longbow-archers.com for information (not in French!) on this peculiar shoot.

Developing a program

Sometimes, archery instructors will be assigned the task of developing an archery program, either from scratch or by modifying an existing one. Why do we make programs? Well, there are several reasons. It gives directors and administrators something concrete to consider when long-range planning for organizations like camps and schools. Similarly, it gives instructors a written outline to follow when planning lessons. Most importantly, though, it tells the students what they can expect to learn, and gets them interested in the program— because without the students, there is no program.

Although not all of these will apply to every organization, in general your program statement should address several key parts:

Program name

It should be simple and self-explanatory, like "Robert Frost Middle School After-School Archery Class". If you are writing a program for a special activity within a larger framework, give it a name that separates it and makes it exciting for the students, like "Advanced Archers" or "Robin's Merry Men."

Program area

Many organizations, such as summer camps, have different departments. Which department will this fall under?

Program duration

List the expected length of the program. This greatly affects what activities you can do; long programs allow more time to complete craft projects and hone archery skills, but require much more planning and can get boring for the students unless you keep introducing fresh activities.

Age of the students

It's important that your activities be suited to age of the student; this is known as age-based programming. Older students will benefit more from complex activities, self-direction, and more in-depth focus on specifics. Younger ones often have short attention spans, and tend to prefer activities where they can pick up the basics quickly. It will take experience, and possibly some trial-and-error, before you have a good feel for what sorts of things different ages can handle.

This is not to say that you can't have a broad mix of ages in your program, but if you do, that should be accommodated by your program as well. You could have activities with a broad appeal, different versions of each activity for each age group, or some other creative solution.

Number of students

Generally, fewer students per instructor is better. The sample lessons talk more about appropriate ratios, and organizations like schools and summer camps have maximum ratios that are dictated by statute or insurance requirements. Sometimes for larger programs, it's possible to get assistants; that helps bring the ratios back down.

Quick overview

Write a sentence or two describing how fun your program will be. It lets administrators know what's planned without having to dive into the details, and it can be used on marketing materials for your camp or school to get students interested. Make it exciting, information-filled, and to the point.

Proposed activities

This is the main body of the program. Here, you list out specific activities with a brief description of each one if it's not obvious. Often, this is a working list, and will get added to or shortened as the program evolves.

Equipment required and anticipated costs

If you need anything special, list it so that administrators can plan for it and you can remember what to collect before the program starts. Depending on your organization, you may be expected to include a budget here as well.

On the following page is an example of an actual proposal for a two-week program of advanced archery that was implemented, with minor modifications, the following year. It doesn't address all of the areas we just talked about, but it's straightforward, simple, and gives everyone —administrators, instructors, and students— something to look at and discuss.

ACTIVITIES

Archery Program Proposal
by Jim Fanjoy (Fletch), Program Specialist

August 22, 2002

Program name: **On Target**
Program focus: Archery
Student age: 11-16
Maximum group size: 16 per session (8 per session preferred)

Summary:
This program will teach archery skills, history, and lore to girls with little to no knowledge of archery, and improve the knowledge base of girls who are already proficient archers.

Suggested Activities:
Construct and use their own arrows.

Construct and use their own archery tackle (finger tabs, arm guards, etc.)

Discuss the history of archery and different styles developed by different cultures.

Watch an archery related movie, such as Robin Hood, or the PBS series "Connections".

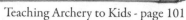

Discuss technical aspects of equipment care & maintenance.

Daily practice sessions to build proficiency, with specific instruction on technique improvement.

Out-trip to a local field archery range.

Special theme shoots and archery games, including:

> watermelon shoot
> silhouette shoots
> stump shooting
> "horse", "follow the leader", etc.
> clout shoot

"Robin Hood"-style archery tournament.

Anticipated Costs:
There shouldn't be many special expenses beyond those for a typical resident camper. I will have a more detailed estimate later in the year. If they make 6 arrows, a bracer, and finger tabs, I think that we can get it done for $20 to $30 per camper.

ACTIVITIES

Archery in Media

The romantic and exciting nature of archery makes it prominent in films, television, comics, art, and literature. These sources can be a great tool for exposing kids to archery. Watch films with them or read stories to them, and then discuss what happened. Some topics to discuss might be:

➳ What kind of a person is the archer? Is he skillful? Does he respect archery as an art? Why does he practice archery?

➳ How do you suppose the subject learned archery?

➳ Why is archery used instead of some other tool, such as a gun or a tennis racket?

➳ What technical things did they get wrong? What did they get right? For example, it's surprising how many artists draw archers with the arrow on the wrong side of the bow.

➳ When does the story take place? Does the archer use the bow because it's all that is available, or because he prefers it? Why?

The following is a small list of archery related entertainment resources. Many others can be found online or at your local library. It's a good idea to review the material before you present it, and decide if a specific title is appropriate to the group you are working with.

The Adventures of Robin Hood (1938): A classic Errol Flynn movie. Though a bit dated, all of the impressive archery effects are real, performed by Howard Hill. They include such things as running stuntmen being shot in the chest[1].

Cavalcade of Archery (1946): A short film displaying the amazing archery skills of Howard Hill, one of the greatest archers of all time.

Robin Hood (1973): This is the Disney version of the famous archery legend. Good for any age.

Connections (1979): James Burke narrates this award-winning historical series. Although the 10 episodes cover a vast range of historical topics, the episode including archery is specifically relevant and especially interesting, if you can find a copy of it.

Robin of Sherwood (1984): A British television miniseries. Careful attention was paid to historical accuracy in equipment, clothes, and tools; especially bows and arrows.

Robin Hood, Prince of Thieves (1991): An exciting portrayal of an excellent

---

1. Amazingly, there were no archery-related injuries during filming.

archer. Violence; not recommended for younger kids.

The Lord of the Rings (2001): An amazing movie trilogy with numerous archery scenes. Though much of it is pure fantasy, the large battle scenes give an accurate impression of what it would be like on a historical battlefield where archery was in play.

The strongest men do not always draw the strongest shot, which thing proveth that drawing strong, lieth not so much in the strength of man, as in the use of shooting. For you shall see a weak smith, which will with a lype and turning of his arm, take up a bar of iron, that another man thrice as strong cannot stir.

-Roger Ascham, 1545

As a rule, nothing does an arrow so much good as to shoot it, and nothing so much harm as to have it lie inactive and crowded in the quiver.
    -Saxton Pope, 1923

Most of your time as an archery instructor will be spent teaching students. Many instructors don't want to mess with equipment maintenance, and it's sort of like changing the oil in your car; you can neglect it for a while without any noticeable ill effects. However, if you ignore the oil in your car too long, you will eventually have to pay a pretty hefty repair bill for a damaged engine. Likewise, if you ignore the maintenance of your archery tackle, you will eventually have to make it up by performing major repairs or replacing items entirely.

DAILY MAINTENANCE

Maintenance of most institutional, camp-style equipment is pretty simple. Before and after each day's shooting, inspect all the equipment for loose or missing parts. Look over each bow for any cracks or fissures. Check the bowstrings for any wear, especially around the servings. If the strings feel dry, rub them with beeswax. That's it.

For more specialized equipment like compound or wooden bows, refer to literature provided by the manufacturer for proper care and feeding.

IT'S BROKEN!

So, what can we do if we find a broken piece of equipment? First off, take it out of service until you can spend some time alone with it. Then, when the teaching sessions are over for the day and you can relax a notch, gather all your broken gear and find a quiet place to work. Luckily, most minor repair tasks are well within the abilities of someone with only the slightest craft skills. You can probably do more than you think you can, so don't be afraid to try some of the harder repairs; at the very least, if you mess it up, it won't be less usable than when you started!

In extreme cases, you might have to throw a piece of badly damaged equipment away. This happens a lot with arrows, for example. I like to save my broken arrows and burn them in the closing campfire at the end of each camp session. This seems like a solemn way to honor them for giving good service, and is also handy because it keeps kids from pulling them out of the

CRAFTS

trash and getting into mischief. In any case, don't forget that you can make new equipment to replace some of the things you've lost... but we'll talk about that in the second part of this section.

Here we have a list of common archery repair jobs, loosely organized from easiest to hardest. So, go to it!

Target faces

Tools needed: tape.

These take a fantastic amount of abuse on the range. Most are paper, and are prone to tearing. You can keep the tearing to a minimum by training your students to hold the paper face when pulling their arrows out, but eventually you will have to repair the faces no matter how careful they are. If you feel so inclined, you can tape over holes and tears with colored tape to match the colors of the rings, but this is generally not worth the effort. You would be better off to leave them torn until it's too ugly or distracting to your archers, then replace them entirely. The good news is that they are inexpensive, and can be easily made by hand. I like to get a few of my more skilled students to make them, in exchange for allowing them extra time on the range.

Target butts

Tools needed: none. Possibly a sailmaker's needle and jute string.

Despite their constant torture, these rarely fail. In the case of hay bale or excelsior butts, they sometimes get really loose and worn out after thousands of arrows. In this case, simply replace them. If a sisal or woven butt should fail, it is worth repairing, but the repair will depend on the damage. The burlap covering can be sewn back together, and the cordage can be sewn back in place with a heavy sailmaker's needle and jute string.

Shafts

Tools needed: none. Possibly an arrow straightener, if using aluminum arrows.

If an arrow shaft is cracked, chipped, or severely warped, there is no choice but to destroy it. It is a danger to anyone who shoots it, because it undergoes a lot of stress every time it is fired, and could snap into sharp, fast splinters when released. There is, however, a minor repair you can make to slightly warped shafts. With wooden shafts, heat the bent area. You can do this by leaving it in the hot sun, rubbing it quickly and repeatedly with a coarse cloth, or even blowing it with a hair dryer. Once it's almost too warm to touch, bend it *gently* in the opposite direction of the bend, and hold it for a few seconds. Release it, and see if it's straight. If not, bend it again, a tiny bit more. Be sure to only bend the area that is crooked or you will make a "C" shaped arrow "S" shaped! It takes some practice to get the hang of this technique, so be patient and keep trying.

Looking along the shaft will give you a good idea if it's straight or not, but the best test is to spin it rapidly. To do this, touch the thumb and middle finger of your left hand together, close to your palm. Holding the arrow point-down, lean the arrow shaft against the nails of these two fingers, just below the fletchings. Let the point of the arrow rest freely in your right palm. Now, blow gently on one of the feathers. The arrow should begin to turn rapidly, making an amusing buzzing noise in the process. If the arrow spins smoothly, it's straight; if it rattles and jumps around, it's still crooked somewhere.

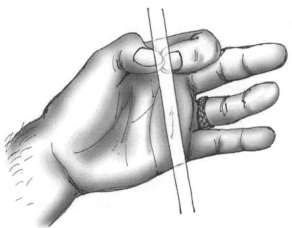

If you are using aluminum arrows, you can straighten them the same way, but the heat isn't needed. There are also commercially available arrow straighteners on the market that look like pliers with round wheels on them; consider investing in one if you use aluminum arrows.

CRAFTS

Arrow points (stamped)

Tools needed: Nail & hammer. Possibly a hand drill & bits, small vise or pliers, and needle nosed pliers.

The cheapest arrows have thin, stamped metal points that are often held in place by crimping. If one should come loose or completely off, you can affix it back in place by placing a nail against the side of the head, and striking it with a hammer. This creates a dimple and depresses the thin metal into the side of the shaft, making the head tight. If you've lost the head

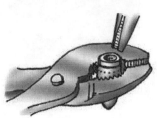

entirely, then you can replace it with a new one, or you can scavenge one from a broken arrow. To do this, clamp the head of the broken arrow gently in a vise or pliers. Cut off the arrow just past the point, then carefully drill out most of the wood with a drill bit that is 1/16" smaller than the diameter of the shaft. With a pair of needle nosed pliers, grab the remaining shaft and wiggle it back and forth, breaking off pieces and pulling them out. Soon you will have a scavenged arrow point you can put on your other shaft as previously described.

Arrow points (cast)

Tools needed: Pliers, ferrule cement, candle.

Higher quality wood arrows have machined points, either field or blunt, that fit on a tapered end of the shaft. They are held in place by a heat sensitive glue called "ferrule cement" that becomes runny when hot, and hard when it cools to room temperature. If these

points come loose or off, you can easily replace them. Hold the point with pliers and heat it over a candle flame until the glue inside runs. Then, force the point back onto the shaft with the pliers (it's too hot to touch at this point). Check that the point is aligned with the shaft before the glue sets, then dunk it in water to cool it quickly and set the glue.

If you should happen to get the head on crooked, not to worry— you can reheat the ferrule cement by holding the point over the fire. When it's hot enough, grab it with the pliers and reposition it until it's where you want it.

Arrow nocks

Tools needed: Pliers, cement, sandpaper, new nocks.

The typical way a nock breaks is by cracking or splitting, in which case it needs to be removed and replaced. Nocks are glued in place, so to get a damaged nock off of a shaft, you will usually need to crush it with pliers to get it to fracture into several small pieces. Then you can pull them off individually with the pliers. Go slowly and gently, being careful not to crush the tapered shaft end underneath. Once all the nock is off, use sandpaper to remove any big chunks of cement, and make the tapered area rough so new cement will stick. Occasionally, nocks just fall off in the course of shooting and are lost. In those cases, sand the exposed tapered end of the shaft and move right on to the next step.

Select a nock that is the proper size for the shaft you are using; the most common sizes are 1/4", 5/16", and 11/32". There are several companies making "archery cement", but anything that will bond both plastic and wood will be acceptable. Lightly coat the taper with cement, and squeeze the new nock on. Now, before the glue sets, **rotate the nock so the string will be perpendicular to the index feather and the grain of the wood.** Also, some nocks have a little bump on one side to make it easier to identify the index feather by feel. If yours do, make sure that the bump on the nock aligns with the index feather.

CRAFTS

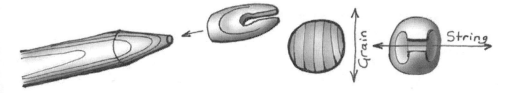

Fletching

Tools needed: sharp knife, sandpaper, fletching cement, pins, feathers. Possibly scissors.

When a feather gets damaged, repairing it is a simple matter. First, look at it and decide if it's worth saving. If it just badly ruffled, you can usually return it to normal by steaming it over a boiling kettle for a few minutes. If some of the beginning or end of the feather is torn away, you can cleanly cut off the tear and put a dab of cement on the wound to hold the now-shorter feather in place. An arrow repaired like this will shoot almost as well as a new one, enough that the difference won't be noticed by beginning archers.

If the feather is seriously mangled, though, you will need to completely remove what is there with a sharp knife. Lay the blade flat against the shaft. Incline it slightly, and then slide it under the feather. It should come off cleanly. Then, roughen the area where the feather used to be with sandpaper, to help the cement adhere better.

Select a feather that is similar in size and shape to the others on the shaft. If you have none that are the right size, you can use a sharp pair of scissors to cut one to match. Also, check to be sure that the new feather is from the same wing as the ones already on the arrow. A "right wing" feather curves left, when viewed from behind the arrow, and vice-versa.

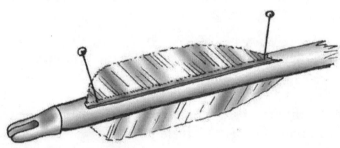

Apply a thin line of cement along the bottom of the vein of the feather, and press it into place where the damaged feather used to be. You can stick a pin through the vein of the feather and into the shaft at the front and back to hold it in place while it dries. Be sure that all the feathers are at the same angle with the shaft, the same distance forward from the nock, and that the fibers of the feather are pointing backwards towards the nock.

This is a pretty quick-and-dirty way to fix fletchings; the subject is treated more thoroughly in this section, under "Making Archery Tackle". You can fix plastic vanes this way, as well, though you will need to use masking tape instead of pins to hold them to aluminum or fiberglass shafts as they dry.

Repairing Archery Tackle

Bracers, tabs, fingers, and other tackle

Tools needed: heavy thread, leather needle

The most common failure with soft tackle like tabs and bracers is when seams or stitching come loose. Repairing them is easy with a needle and thread. Sew through the holes where the broken thread used to be, making a new seam. If the tear or break was not on a seam, you can usually stitch the torn parts back together with sturdy thread, and return the item to service. Cloth and leather repair techniques could take up an entire book to themselves, so I won't go into it here, but the important thing to remember is that you can fix almost any broken leather or cloth item if you have the time and patience.

Bowstrings

Tools Needed: none (a cake of beeswax, for old-style strings)

When the string beginneth to wear, trust it not; but away with it,
for it is an ill saved halfpenny that costs a man a crown.
  -Roger Ascham, 1545

Modern bowstrings made from synthetics like B-50 Dacron and FastFlight typically require little maintenance beyond regular inspection for excess wear. However, more traditional bowstrings made with natural fibers like linen must be waxed regularly to maintain their strength and keep out moisture. To do this, rub them with a cake of beeswax, then rub the string back and forth with a cloth several times. The heat from the friction melts the wax and works it into the bowstring.

When a bowstring becomes worn, it needs to be replaced. Repair is not an option, because if a string should actually break when in use, it could be harmful to both the archer and the bow. Before each day's shooting, examine the entire string for frayed or worn areas and broken fibers. *Serving* is the extra cord reinforcing wrapped around the bowstring at the loops and the middle; pay special attention to the bowstring where it contacts the bow or arrow. If you find a worn or damaged string, cut it up immediately to prevent someone who doesn't know better from accidentally using it later.

When you order a new string for your bow, look for the bow's information label; it's usually on the riser or belly of one of the limbs. The

CRAFTS

label will have the two pieces of information you need: the draw weight, in pounds, and the string length, in inches. When you read the bow's label and place the order, be aware that there is a difference between AMO length and actual string length. Generally, most bows and string manufacturers work in AMO length, but if you have to convert (or measure an existing string), AMO length roughly equals the actual length of the string plus 4".

You can also make your own strings from scratch without too much difficulty; there are instructions later in this section if you're interested. It might be worth reading anyway for more information about string sizes, allowable poundage, materials, etc.

Compound bows are a special situation. If your string is attached to the cables by double teardrops, you can replace the string with the help of a friend. Draw the bow, and hold it at full draw while your friend attaches the new bowstring to the empty side of the teardrops. Let the bow down slowly, so that both strings are in place. Then, draw the bow again by the new string. Hold it at full draw, while your friend removes the old string (which is now loose). Gently let the bow down, and you're done. If your compound bow **doesn't** have double teardrops, then you will need a bow press to change the string. Unless you happen to have one and know how to use it, take the bow to an archery shop.

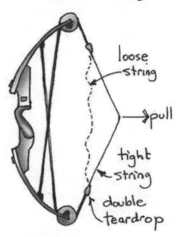

loose string

pull

tight string

double teardrop

Installing nocking point indicators

Tools needed: Bowsquare, nocking point indicator, nocking pliers. Or dental floss and glue.

Installing a nocking point indicator on the bowstring is the single easiest thing you can do to improve an archer's precision. The nocking point indicator is a tiny clip of brass with a plastic liner inside to protect the string. When clamped in place, it gives the archer a fixed location to nock their arrow, ensuring consistency. It's important to locate it correctly, though.

First, you need to find a point on the string that is exactly perpendicular to the top of the arrow rest or shelf. A *bowsquare* is a tool custom designed for this job and clips to the string to make it easier, but if you are careful, you can also use a drafting triangle or anything you know has an exact right angle. Once you've found the perpendicular point, move up the string 1/8" and place a mark. This is where the bottom of the arrow should line up when nocked. If you have nocks that are the full width of the arrow, then move up the string again one arrow diameter. This the top of the shaft, where you want the BOTTOM of the nocking point indicator to be located. Take the nocking point pliers and clamp the nocking point indicator onto the string at this point.

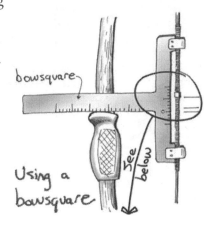

If your arrows have nocks that are skinnier than the arrow, your nocking point indicator will need to be slightly lower, equal to the distance of the offset of the nock. The overall result we are going for is to have the arrow as perpendicular to the string as possible, because that ensures the straightest flight and most efficient use of the bow's energy. Then, we move the nock up 1/8". This gives us a margin of

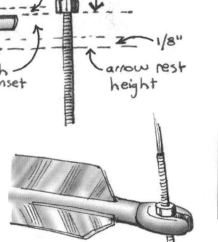

error in case the nocking point shifts a little or the string stretches over time, because if the nocking point is ever lower than the perpendicular point, the back of the arrow will bang against the rest and cause a wobbly flight. If it's a little high, the only ill effect you get is an imperceptible loss in efficiency.

To use the nocking point indicator, simply nock the arrow to the string beneath the nocking point, and then slide the arrow up the string until snug.

CRAFTS

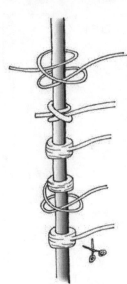

Although special nocking point pliers are cheap, you can make do with regular pliers if you are careful not to pinch or cut the string. If you can't afford a pack of nocking point indicators, you can make one from dental floss. Tie a few clove hitches around the string at the point you would have installed the metal clip, and wrap enough floss around the string to stop the arrow from sliding any higher. Tie off with a few more clove hitches, and place a dab of glue or epoxy on it to keep it from unraveling while shooting.

Bows

A bow full drawn is seven-eighths broken.
-Thomas Waring, 1832

In general, bow repairs are beyond the call of duty for most archers. Typical bow damage includes cracking, compression fractures (they look like raised lines on the belly of the bow, like the frets of a guitar), delamination, and (in wood bows) dents. If you discover a damaged bow, remove it from service immediately. Tape a big paper note to it that says "damaged" so that no one finds it later and accidentally shoots it, risking injury. Deal with the damaged bow as soon as possible. Some bows, such as those of wood or natural products, are only good for firewood once they are damaged. Others, like compound bows, can be repaired, but these repairs need to be performed by a skilled technician. Refer to the manufacturer's literature.

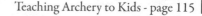

Every field archer should make his own tackle. If he cannot make and repair it, he will never shoot very long, because it is in constant need of repair.
  -Saxton Pope, 1923

Although making archery equipment with kids might sound a little wacky at first, it's not all that difficult, and can add a lot to an archer's experience. You don't need a lot of fancy equipment or special skills for most archery craft projects. Making tackle gives any archer a way to stay in the sport when the weather turns foul, and for kids, it also gives them a quiet time to relax and talk with you while they work. By making your own archery gear, you're taking part in an ancient ritual: grandfathers by the fireside showing their grandchildren how to trim fletchings, the Native American sitting on the high plains as he flakes arrowheads, the medieval English bowyer as he tillers yew staves in his stone cottage. There is romance and mystery in making these things, and young archers should be exposed to crafting as well.

Tools and materials required are listed under each project, so be sure you have everything you need before starting. When teaching these crafts to new archers, it's best to try it alone the first time. Not only does this help you stay calm when things don't seem to be going as planned, but you can also measure how long an activity might take and double check that you have all the tools and materials you need. This section contains activities roughly organized from easiest to hardest, so if you're unsure of your skills, start with projects closer to the front of the section and then work your way down.

CRAFTS

TARGET FACES
Tools needed: Scissors, string, pushpins. Possibly an
  old yardstick and hand drill.
Materials used: Butcher paper, markers, paint.

This is one of the easiest projects in all of archery, and also one of the most popular with kids. The basic procedure is simple: you cut off a piece off paper large enough for your target, or for larger faces, splice several pieces together with tape on the back. Then, you draw the target out with markers and color it with paint. Tempera paint is inexpensive, easy to clean, and works well— unless you are going to leave your target faces in the rain.

If so, you might want to use a waterproof paint. The same can be said for markers.

There are a lot of different face designs, so we'll start with the simplest. The traditional target face has concentric, colored rings. From the center out, they are gold, red, blue, black, and white (a hundred years ago, the blue ring was also white[1]). Sometimes, each ring has a thin black like down the center so the scores can be broken down further. The overall size of an 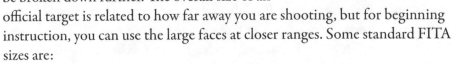 official target is related to how far away you are shooting, but for beginning instruction, you can use the large faces at closer ranges. Some standard FITA sizes are:

Overall diameter	Width per ring
48" (122cm)	4.8" (12cm)
32" (80cm)	3.2" (8cm)
24" (60cm)	2.4" (6cm)
16" (40cm)	1.6" (4 cm)

The best way to make uniform circles is with a compass. On the larger faces, you will need to make a special large compass. This can be done by drilling six holes in an old yardstick. They should be large enough to stick a marker tip through, and spaced evenly apart at the same distance as the rings you want to draw for your target.

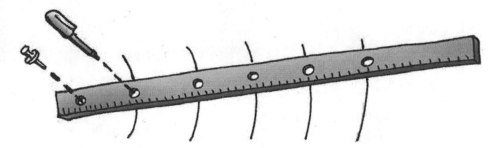

To draw perfect circles with a marker, place your paper on a flat board or craft table, and stick a pushpin through the center. Then, place the first

---

1. Going even farther back, targets before 1687 had only 4 concentric rings instead of 5, and only the center gold was specifically colored. (Soar, p. 142)

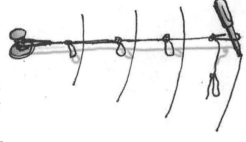

hole of your yardstick compass over the pushpin. Put a marker through the next hole, and draw a circle by spinning the yardstick around the pushpin. Repeat this procedure until you have all five rings drawn. Color the rings, and you're done.

If you can't make a yardstick compass, you can get by with a "measuring string" as a compass to guide you with each circle, keeping the string taught all the way around. Make a measuring string by tying a loop at one end to slip over the tack, and add five other loops spaced at even intervals along the string. You will have to take care and experiment some to get the loops evenly spaced and in exactly the right place, and it helps to have a different measuring string for each given target size you might want to draw.

There are many target face designs, so here's a few that you can start with. After that, experiment!

CRAFTS

illustration by Frank Victoria

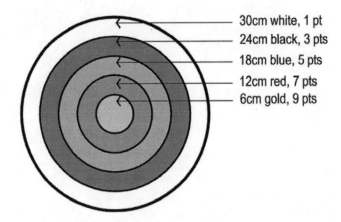

30cm white, 1 pt
24cm black, 3 pts
18cm blue, 5 pts
12cm red, 7 pts
6cm gold, 9 pts

FITA face: This is the standard face used for international competition. It comes in many equally-proportioned sizes; the one shown here is the 24" face. On some faces, the rings are divided with a thin black line; if so, then the inner ring of each color is one point higher. Often, with young archers, I simplify the scoring by only using the colored rings and making it 5 points for a gold down to 1 for a white.

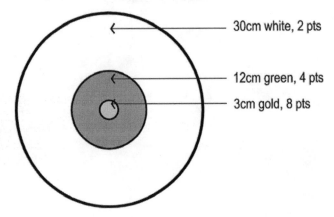

30cm white, 2 pts

12cm green, 4 pts
3cm gold, 8 pts

Luttrell face: This medieval target face is the earliest on record, and can be seen in the Luttrell Psalter, a book written in the early 1300s. Though its exact size of this target is not known, several reenactment societies have made modern versions of it. The gold in the center was originally a wooden peg used to hold the target face to the butt. You can make it with a compass set for 3cm, 12cm, and 30cm for the three circles, or you can lay a new piece of butcher paper over a 24" FITA face and trace the outer circle, the outside of the red ring, and the inner gold.

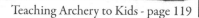

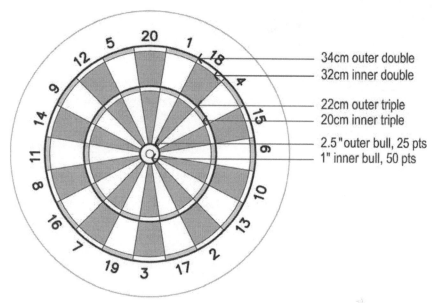

- 34cm outer double
- 32cm inner double
- 22cm outer triple
- 20cm inner triple
- 2.5" outer bull, 25 pts
- 1" inner bull, 50 pts

Dartchery face: Basically a dart board drawn on paper, this is all you need to play Dartchery (see the section on Activities). If you enlarge the face to twice the size they use for darts, it is very shootable. Draw the circles with a compass using the sizes shown, then use a protractor to divide the face into 20-degree wedges. Write the point values of each wedge around the outer circle with a marker.

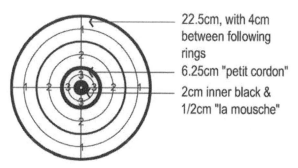

- 22.5cm, with 4cm between following rings
- 6.25cm "petit cordon"
- 2cm inner black & 1/2cm "la mousche"

Beursault face: Traditionally, a special target face is used for Beursault (see the section on Activities for a description of this type of shooting). This black-and-white target is pretty small for the 57 yard range it is normally shot at, but you can make one yourself and shoot at it from shorter ranges just for fun.

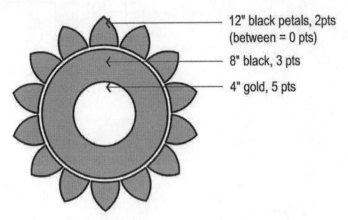

12" black petals, 2pts
(between = 0 pts)

8" black, 3 pts

4" gold, 5 pts

d'Anjou tournament face: I enjoy shooting at this fanciful target for a change of pace. It's loosely based on the the face from *Robin of Sherwood*, one of my favorite programs. The potential to hit between the flower petals and still score a "miss" while on the paper appeals to my capricious nature, and encourages a more concentrated effort at staying in the bull.

Animal face: These are extremely popular for hunting, but they could also be useful for beginning archers, because they teach concentration and get the archer used to thinking about exactly where on the target their arrow will land, rather than shooting at the entire target as a whole. Animals can be sketched by hand, or you can tape the target paper to a wall and trace a picture of an animal from an overhead projector.

Monster face: Similar to the animal face, this is just a drawing of a fanciful monster, to add some variety.

BRACER (ARMGUARD)

Tools needed: Heavy-duty leather shears or a razor
knife, leather punch, leather awl (optional),
needle (optional).

Materials used: Thick leather, waxed thread. Elastic cord, shoelace, Velcro,
or some other closure.

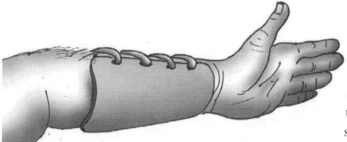

A bracer
is essential
to beginning
archers, to keep
them from being
slapped by the
bowstring. But more advanced users can
benefit from them as well, because they help keep your sleeve out of the path
of the bowstring. Bracers have been around since prehistoric times, so the
technique for making them isn't very sophisticated; in fact, you could even
tape a piece of curled cardboard to your forearm in a pinch. But a quality
bracer is easy to make, will last for years, and is a great opportunity for your
students to exercise their creativity.

Cutting out

Photocopy the bracer pattern on the next page, and cut it out. Trace it
onto a piece of thick leather, and cut that out with leather shears. For the
lace-up type of bracer, punch out all the holes with a leather punch about
¼" in diameter. If you're using straps with buckles or Velcro, transfer the "X"
marks from the pattern to the leather, but don't punch any holes.

Curling & forming

Soak the bracer in warm
water for a few minutes, then
curl it to match the shape of
your forearm. Let it dry in this
curled position. You can place
it between two heavy objects
(soda cans, rocks, bricks, etc.) to
hold it in shape until it dries.

CRAFTS

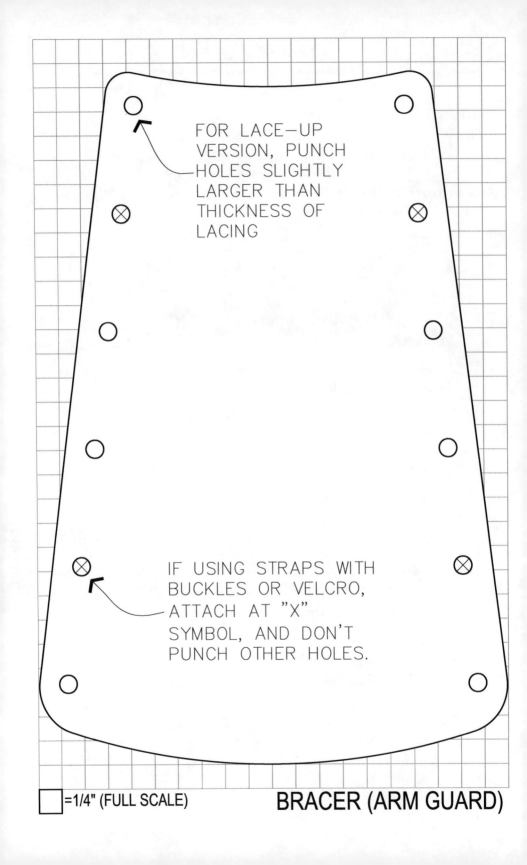

FOR LACE—UP
VERSION, PUNCH
HOLES SLIGHTLY
LARGER THAN
THICKNESS OF
LACING

IF USING STRAPS WITH
BUCKLES OR VELCRO,
ATTACH AT "X"
SYMBOL, AND DON'T
PUNCH OTHER HOLES.

☐ =1/4" (FULL SCALE)

BRACER (ARM GUARD)

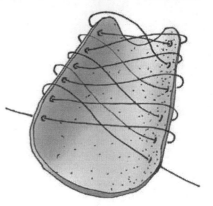

Lacing

Lace up the bracer in a zigzag pattern. If you use cord or leather lace, leave enough extra that the bracer can be tied when it's laced tightly. If you use elastic cord, you won't need this extra length, and you can also get the bracer on and off easier. Some archers prefer straps instead of lacing; ½" wide straps of leather or heavy cloth work well. Attach them to the bracer by sewing or riveting where the pattern is marked with an "X". These straps should have an adjustable connector like Velcro or a buckle.

Decorating & embellishment

The big, flat area of the bracer is great for decoration; many examples of elaborately embellished bracers have survived from as far back as the 16th century[2]. You can experiment with leather carving, painting, dying, or stamping to create a personalized bracer of your own.

FINGER PROTECTION

Tools needed: Heavy-duty scissors or a razor knife, leather awl, needle

Materials used: Leather, waxed thread. Possibly a keychain ring.

Repeated shooting of any but the lightest bows will eventually make your fingers sore. Good finger protection will be thick enough to keep away blisters, yet thin enough to allow the archer to properly feel the string and arrow. Supple, smooth, crease-free protection will also help give a smooth release. The simplest and oldest[3] finger protection is a tab, or specially cut piece of flat leather. More elaborate protection like "fingers" or a half-glove are easier to use, but some archers complain that they are uncomfortable in hot weather. You can make either type fairly easily.

CRAFTS

---

2.   The *Mary Rose*, wrecked in 1545, contained at least two dozen bracers decorated with images or words.

3.   In Coventry, England an archaeologist discovered a child's archery tab dating from the early 1500s. (Soar, p.128)

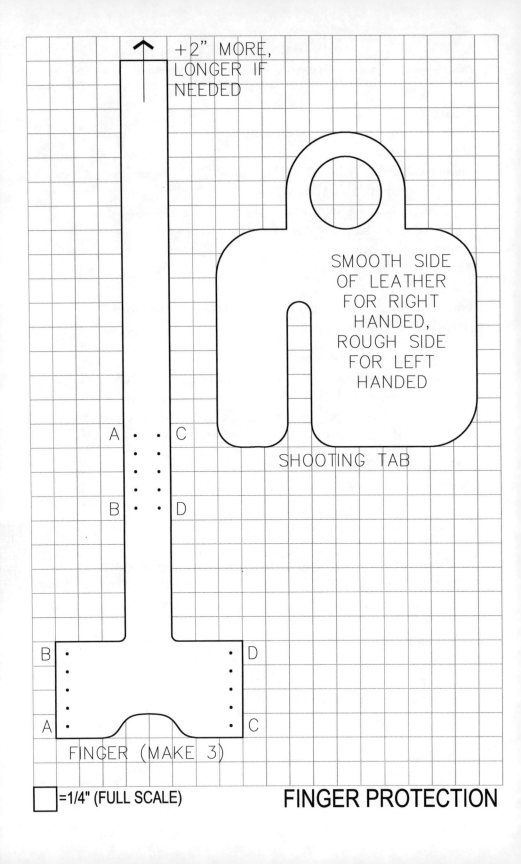

+2" MORE, LONGER IF NEEDED

SMOOTH SIDE OF LEATHER FOR RIGHT HANDED, ROUGH SIDE FOR LEFT HANDED

SHOOTING TAB

A · · C

B · · D

B · · · · D

A · · · · C

FINGER (MAKE 3)

☐ =1/4" (FULL SCALE)

FINGER PROTECTION

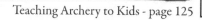

Making the tab

Photocopy the pattern on the facing page, and cut it out. Trace it onto a piece of medium-weight leather, with the smooth side of the leather facing up for a right handed tab, or the flesh side up for a left-handed tab. Cut the shape out with heavy duty scissors or a razor knife. That's it. You're done. To use the tab, stick your right middle finger through the hole, and curl your three shooting fingers around to touch the flesh side of the leather.

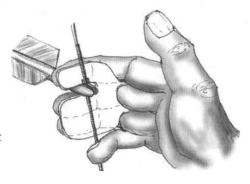

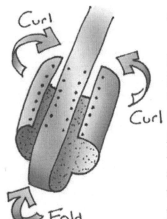

Curl

Curl

Fold

Cutting out the fingers

To make a more elaborate set of fingers, photocopy the finger pattern on the facing page, and cut it out. Trace it onto a piece of thin leather three times, making the end with the arrow at least two inches longer than the pattern shows. You might even need to make it longer than that, depending on the size of the archer's hand. Experiment a little. Cut out the three leather fingers, and use the leather awl to poke holes in the leather where the black dots are shown on the pattern.

CRAFTS

Sewing the fingers

Using the needle and thread, sew two seams through the holes on each finger, matching letter A to A, B to B, and so on. Put the fingers on each of your three shooting fingers, and mark the tail where it crosses the middle of the back of your

Sew

hand. Take them back off, fold the tail at the mark, and sew the tail down around the key ring (see illustration on the next page). If you don't have a key ring, you can use a loop of cord, or you can cut out a circle of leather about the same size as the key ring.

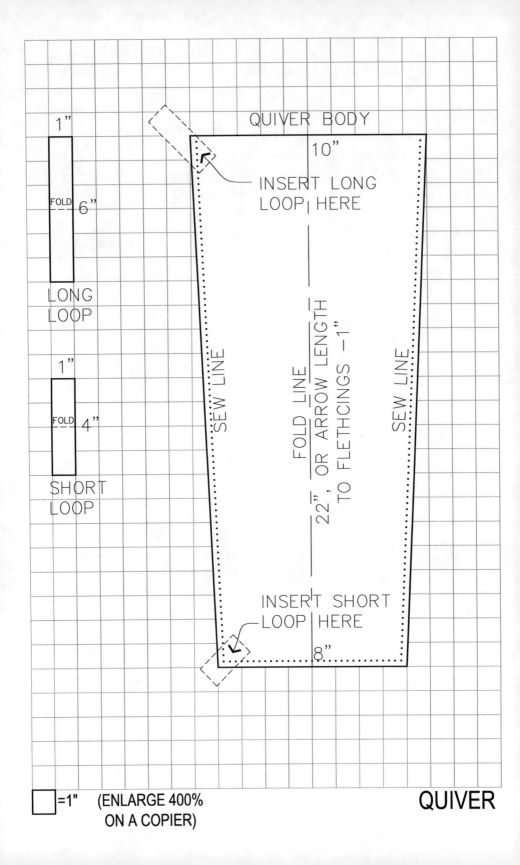

QUIVER

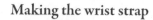
Making the wrist strap

To keep the fingers in place, you need a wrist strap. You can make one from two half-inch wide strips of leather about eight inches long, fastened to the key chain in the same way as the fingers. Simply tie them around your wrist, and you're ready to go. Or, you could add a Velcro closure, snap, toggle, buckle... this is an opportunity to exercise your creativity.

QUIVER

Tools needed: Heavy-duty scissors or a razor knife, leather awl, needle

Materials used: Medium weight leather or heavy cloth, waxed thread. Possibly a strap or belt. Alternate version: cardboard tube, strapping tape, cord.

A quiver is useful for holding and protecting your arrows when you are out in the field, and also makes a convenient place to store them when you aren't shooting. This pattern is for a simple quiver that can hang from your belt (in the medieval or modern style) or from your back (as they did in the Victorian era and early 1900s.) There are a million variations on this basic design, so feel free to experiment. The only real requirement is that the quiver not be so long that the fletchings are covered and get ruffled when you remove an arrow.

Cut out the pattern

Mark the pattern onto a piece of leather or heavy cloth, such as canvas. The size shown works for most arrows, but you can customize the quiver for a specific arrow length by making it the same length as the distance from your arrow point to the fletchings, minus an inch. Once you've marked the pattern, cut out the body and the two loops.

CRAFTS

Sew it up

Fold the body of the quiver in half, and sew it along the bottom and side. If you're using leather, you will probably have to pre-punch holes in the leather with an awl. As you are sewing, pause at the corner and the top end so you can insert the folded over loops and sew them in place at the same time.

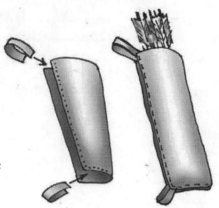

Add a belt or strap

You can now wear the quiver on your hip by passing the belt through the loop at the top of the quiver. If you add a strap between the two loops, you can wear it slung over your shoulder.

Alternate version

You can make a simple, temporary belt quiver with everyday household items you can scrounge up. First, measure your arrows from the point to the start of the fletchings. Find a cardboard tube from wrapping paper or something similar, and cut a section of it to match the length you just measured. Tape one end closed. At the other end, punch a hole in the cardboard near the top. Pass a cord through it, tie it to your belt, and you're ready to shoot in less than five minutes.

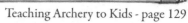

BOWSTRINGS: CONTINUOUS LOOP

Wax is to an archer as tar is to a sailor; use it often, and always have two strings to your bow.
-Saxton Pope, 1923

Tools needed: Scissors, hammer, nails, 6' piece of lumber (or a long workbench). Optional string serving jig is very handy.
Materials used: B50 Dacron thread, nylon serving thread, epoxy

A damaged bowstring is dangerous to repair, and should be thrown away. But it's easy to make a new one from scratch to replace it! Before you start on a bowstring, read the description of different types and materials in the Equipment: Bow section. For our first example, we'll make a continuous-loop Dacron string. These are the most common on modern archery equipment, perform really well, are very reliable, and are the easiest to make. Afterwards, we will talk a little about Flemish strings, in case you want to do something fancier and a little more artistic.

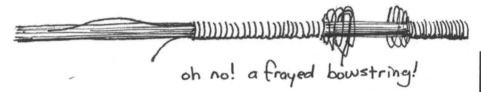

oh no! a frayed bowstring!

Sizing the string

The first thing you must do is find out the requirements of the string, in terms of length and number of strands. If you have an existing string that you know works, you can just copy it by measuring the distance between the loops, and counting the number of strands in the string. If not, then you will need to read the label on the bow. To find the loop-to-loop length of your new string, take the AMO length and subtract four inches. The number of strands required[4] is equal to the following chart:

---

4.   This bowstring strand chart is compiled from many often-conflicting sources. The serious student of archery would be well advised to do additional research into this subject.

CRAFTS

Bow Weight	B-50 Dacron	FastFlight	#12 Linen[5]
Up to 25#	8	14	18
25-35#	10	16	24
35-45#	12	18	30
45-55#	14	20	36
55-65#	16		60[6]
65-75#	16		

*If the string manufacturer publishes different numbers, use them.

Adding additional strands increases the strength of the bowstring, but will reduce the speed of the string somewhat, giving your arrow less power. I recommend you use B50 Dacron for all your institutional strings, because Fastflight is so stiff it might damage older bows, and linen is a traditional material that requires a lot of wax and maintenance.

Setting up

Once you know the size of your string, you need to set up a jig. Commercial stringmaking jigs are available, but it's cheaper to simply drive two large finish nails into a board or workbench, spaced the same distance apart as the length of your string.

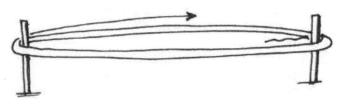

Winding the string

Wrap the end of the Dacron around the first nail a few times to keep it from moving, then start making large loops of Dacron from one nail to the other. Go around enough times to build up the number of strands you want for your string (each complete loop equals two strands). Cut the spool off leaving a few extra inches. Then, unwrap the start of the string from the nail and tie the two loose ends together, leaving as little slack as possible in your loops. Now you have what is known as a "continuous loop". Trim the loose ends, leaving about half an inch or so.

---

5. Use only the highest quality Irish shoemaker's linen. String quantities are divisible by three because linen usually appears only on Flemish strings, due to their historical character. Most of these values are from Shane p.57.

6. Howard Hill used #13 string, and felt that one strand per pound of draw weight was better. This might be worth considering on high-poundage bows.

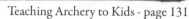

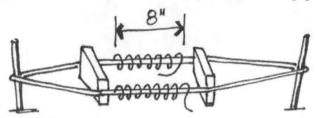

Serving the nock loops

Rotate the entire continuous loop around so that the knot is exactly halfway between the two nails. Stick two small blocks of wood or empty thread spools between each side of the bowstring, to hold them about four inches apart. We will now wind eight inches of nylon serving string around one bundle of Dacron strings, starting four inches to the left of the knot and moving right. Start your serving with a clove-hitch as shown below, and hold the loose end against the Dacron so it becomes buried underneath the servings as you work.

After about seven inches, stop and place a loop of spare thread against the Dacron as shown below. Continue serving until you have eight inches total, then tie off with another clove hitch. Snip off the serving thread, leaving about two inches. Pass the trailing end of the serving through the loop you made, then pull the free ends of the loop to drag the last of the serving line beneath itself. Snip off any remaining string, and repeat this process to serve the other half of the bowstring.

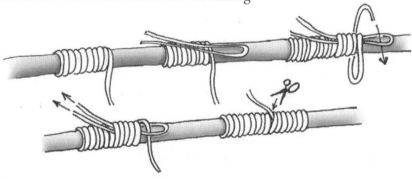

CRAFTS

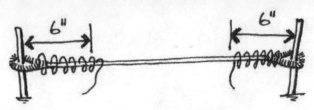

Closing the nock loops

Remove the string spacers and rotate the continuous loop back again to its original position, so the nock servings you just made will be centered over the nails. Move now to the ends of the bowstring. Starting about an inch out from the nail, start serving as before, wrapping both halves of the bowstring and moving away from the nail. When you are about five inches out, stop and lay a loop of scrap Dacron against the bowstring. Continue wrapping one more inch and finish off the serving like before.

Traditionally, one loop of the bowstring is left larger than the other. This makes it easier to readily identify which end is up when stringing the bow, so your nocking point indicator is in the right place. You will need to experiment some to see what size loops fit best on your bows.

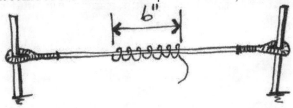

Serving the center

Note the center of the string, and move about three inches to the left. Begin serving around the entire bundle of Dacron strands, moving to the right in the same fashion as before. Continue serving until you have five inches, then insert a Dacron loop, wrap one more inch, and finish off as before.

Finishing up

Place small dots of epoxy on the exposed ends of each serving, to help prevent fraying. Let the string sit on the jig until dry. When you test it on the bow for the first time, consolidate and protect the bowstring by rubbing the Dacron strands with a little wax and a clean cloth.

String serving jig

Though not necessary, this inexpensive tool is a great timesaver. It holds a spool of serving thread and has a little rider that hangs on the bowstring. When serving, it dispenses thread as you spin it around the bowstring. With a little practice and a quick wrist-action, you can twirl it around the bowstring, serving eight inches of string in under a minute.

BOWSTRINGS: FLEMISH
Tools needed: Scissors.
Materials used: B50 Dacron thread, nylon serving thread, epoxy, beeswax

This is a more historical bowstring design, based on the much-sought-after strings that came out of Flanders in the middle ages. You still see Flemish-style strings today on longbows and in historical reenactments. It is strong, adjustable for more than one size of bow, and quite attractive. You can even make it from two colors of string, giving it a candy cane appearance! However, its drawbacks are that it is higher maintenance: Flemish strings needs to be adjusted carefully for correct fistmele, and must be broken in to reduce stretching. So, how do we make one?

Cutting the strings
Based on the previous chart, decide how many strands your bowstring will have. Round up so your total is evenly divisible by three. Cut that number of strings, each equal to the actual length of your bow plus 12 inches, and separate them into three groups. If you want, you can create a fancy bowstring by using different color string for each group.

Preparing the groups
Rub the first and last 12 inches of all the strands with beeswax, to help them stick together. In each separate group, stagger the ends of the strands over the first two inches, then twist the first eight inches of each group in your hand, to get them to all stick together into a rope of sorts.

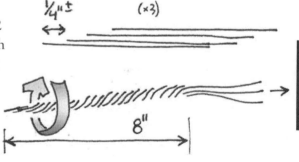

Starting the plait
Bring all three groups together about four inches from the end. One at a time, twist each group to the right a turn and lay it to the left

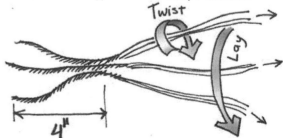

CRAFTS

over the others. Repeat this process until you have about two inches of twisted string. If you have ever made rope, this is essentially the same process.

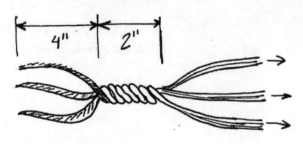

Making the top loop

Now, fold over the twisted, ropey part so that the four inch long free ends are laying alongside the long strings. Rub each string against its partner so they stick together with the wax, then continue the twist-and-lay plait you were doing earlier. Stop when you get down to single groups of strings again.

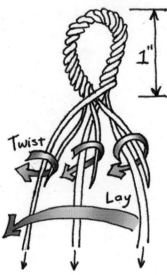

Plaiting the bowstring

The top loop is finished, so hook it over something convenient like a nail, cup hook, or your grandma's big toe. Pull the three groups out so they are straight, and set two aside. Take the third between the palms of your hand, and roll it to the right (same direction as before) several times until it's twisted fairly tightly, and balls up if you don't hold tension on it. Tape it down in the stretched position, and repeat this process with the other two groups. Now, here's the tricky bit: Grab the ends of all three groups in your hand, hold them high over your head, and unhook the loop from whatever is holding it. If you twisted everything enough times in the correct direction, the bowstring should dance around for a bit and turn into a long, twisted rope. Sometimes it helps to hold a little tension on the loop end by attaching a weight.

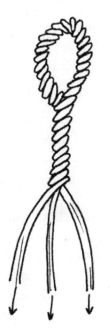

Cleaning up the bottom

The remaining end of the bowstring is usually not very tight, so give each group some extra turns and smooth them together into a tight rope. If they don't stick well, add some extra wax.

Tying the timber hitch

The bottom of the string is tied onto the bow with a timber hitch. Tie it by wrapping the loose end of the bowstring into a loop then back around itself several times, as shown in the picture. When you place it into the lower string nock of the bow, pull it tight and it will cinch up around the bow.

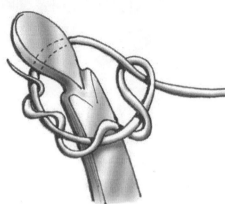

Stretching and adjusting the string

String the bow, and pull it gently a few times to stretch the string. Check the fistmele (brace height): it should be equal to that recommended for the bow, or if none is known, the distance from the base of your fist to the top of your thumb. You can adjust the fistmele by retying the timber hitch up or down the bowstring, and you can make slight adjustments of a half-inch or so by taking the top loop off the bow and twisting or untwisting the bowstring. Once you have the fistmele right, shoot the bow several times before you add a nocking point indicator. During the first few days of use, the string will stretch slightly as is settles into its new shape, and you might have to reposition your nocking point. When the bow is unstrung, the timber hitch is usually left in place.

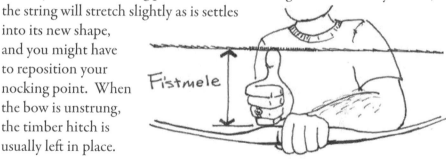

Fistmele

Serving

Apply serving to the center of the bowstring string the same way you would for a continuous-loop string. No serving is required on the top loop, because it is already very strong, being twice as thick as that of a continuous-loop bowstring.

SERVING WITHOUT GLUE

There is another way to tie frayproof servings onto bowstrings, without using glue. It's a little more complicated, but once you master it, you can apply the technique elsewhere, like whipping the ends of ropes, or making tied-on fletchings.

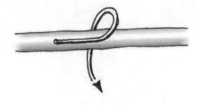

Take the serving string, and lay about an inch along the bowstring.

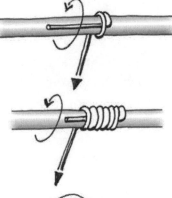

Hold it in place with your fingers as you wrap a few turns of serving around the bowstring, holding the first inch in place.

After a few wraps, pull it tight.

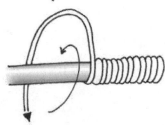

Continue to wrap the serving, covering the entire starting end of the serving string and progressing down the bowstring until you are about an inch from the point at which you'd like to stop.

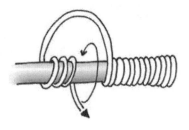

Now, pull out a big loop of serving string, large enough to pass your serving spool through. Resume wrapping the serving around the bowstring, in the same direction, but INSIDE the loop you just made. I use my left index finger to hold the loop open, but you could hang a little weight off of the loop, or have a friend hold it open for you.

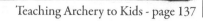

Once you've wrapped about an inch of serving inside the loop, pull a few more inches of serving string off the spool, and cut it. With your thumb and forefinger, hold the end of the serving string against the part of the bowstring that you've already served.

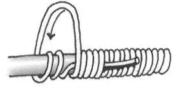

Wrap more serving string over the top of the loose end, using up string from the loop.

When you've used up all the serving string inside the loop, pull the loose end until the serving is tight.

Cut off the remaining serving string as close to the serving as you can.

Adding a drop of glue over the ends of the serving doesn't hurt, but usually isn't necessary when they're tied this way. With practice, you will be able to tie this quickly and get a tight, even serving that won't unravel.

CRAFTS

ARROWS

To make a hunting arrow requires about an hour, and one should be willing to look for one almost this time when it is lost.
   -Dr. Saxton Pope, 1923

The Doctor says it takes about an hour to make a good arrow. I can add that it takes about four hours to make a bad one.
   -Stewart White, 1923

<u>Tools Required</u>: Fletching jig, taper tool, small saw, candle, pliers, clothespins (optional), steel wool (optional)

<u>Materials needed</u>: Shafts, points, nocks, feathers, glue (Duco™ works well), ferrule cement. Polyurethane wood sealer and paints are recommended but not required.

Making arrows, from an economic standpoint, it not a great idea for educational programs. For the cost of the materials and tools required, you could buy three times as many finished arrows, ready for shooting, and save yourself a lot of time in the process. But the art of the fletcher still holds magic, and making arrows is a worthwhile activity to teach kids: it gives them a sense of accomplishment, and they have something tangible they can take home with them at the end of the day. In one of my advanced camp programs, every student gets to make (and keep) an arrow of their own, so they can truly learn all of the steps involved.

There are many subtle nuances to good arrowmaking, and there are entire books on the subject. Here we'll only cover the fundamentals of making a serviceable, camp-quality arrow. If you are making many arrows, it's easiest to do them in assembly-line fashion, performing the same procedure on every arrow before moving to the next step. If you are teaching kids, it's best to give each their own arrow parts, and have them follow along with you as you make an arrow of your own from start to finish.

Material selection

The materials you need for your arrow will be affected greatly by what the arrow is going to be used for, and what level of quality you want. Shaft materials, fletching types, point styles, and other options are explained in the "Equipment: Arrow" section at the beginning of the book. For this example, I am going to assume that we'll be making an inexpensive, lightweight target arrow for use by summer camp archers.

For shafts, choose wooden shafts intended for arrow use, such as Port Orford cedar, Sitka spruce, or Douglas fir. Spine weights come in five-pound groups; select a shaft that matches the draw weight of the bows your students are shooting. Prices will vary depending on your geographic location and what trees are being harvested, so shop around. Avoid the temptation to purchase dowels at a lumber yard; they aren't graded to the same quality standards as arrow shafts and might contain dangerous defects.

Tapered field points are useful in the most shooting situations, and are the easiest to install; for students, buy the lightest ones available (usually 100 grain). Plastic nocks come in all sorts of pretty colors, and you can sometimes get a deal if you call an archery shop and offer to buy their random extra colors.

When selecting feathers, shape and color have little impact on performance and are matters of personal preference. Three-inch feathers are adequate for light target arrows, but heavier arrows using field points (or any other heavy point) should have four- or five-inch feathers. "Left-wing" or "right-wing" indicates which side of the bird they came from[7], but doesn't affect their shooting qualities. Be warned, however, that if your fletching jig is the helical type, you will need feathers that are the same handedness as your jig.

Seal the shaft

This first step is optional, but makes nicer arrows that are resistant to dirt and moisture. Rub the shaft with steel wool until smooth. Pour a little polyurethane sealer into a

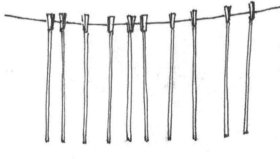

rag, and rub the shaft until it's coated with a thin layer of sealer. Clip the end of the shaft to a clothesline and let air-dry overnight. For a nicer finish, you can repeat this process one or two more times.

---

7.   For some reason, left-wing feathers are often less expensive. Rumor has it that turkey farms clip the right wing to make it easier to handle the turkeys, so there are less right wing feathers available to suppliers.

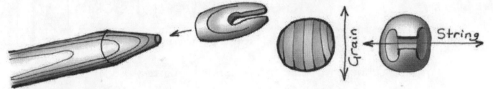

Install the nock

Using the taper tool as you would a pencil sharpener, shave one end of the shaft into a point. Taper tools have two different angles: 5° for points, and a wider 11° for nocks. We'll do the nock side first, so use the wider angle. Once your shaft is tapered, place a little Duco cement on the taper, then twist on a nock. Before the glues sets, rotate the nock so that the slot is perpendicular to the grain of the wood, as shown in the illustration. This ensures that the strongest axis of the arrow will be aligned with the direction of bend[8] when fired (see *archer's paradox* in the Lore section for more info).

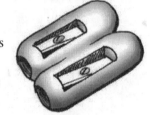

Size the shaft

Every good arrow is custom-fit to the archer. An arrow that is too long has unnecessary weight, and an arrow that is too short poses a risk of draw-through and injuring the archer.[9] The easiest way to check arrow length is to have the archer take the full-length shaft and place the nock against the pit

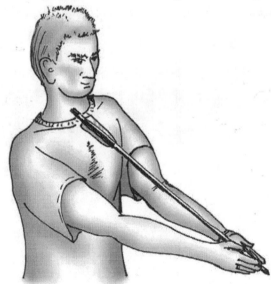

at the base of their throat. Then, have them stretch their arms out in front of them as far as possible, palms open and towards each other, with the arrow shaft in between. The farthest point they can reach on the shaft is the ideal length of the arrow. Mark it with a pencil and cut the shaft off at this point with a saw.

---

8. As an interesting side note, when arrows are measured for spine weight, they are tested with the grain aligned parallel to the measuring apparatus as well.

9. When shot, a longer arrow will also bend more than a short arrow, all else being equal. Again, this relates to Archer's Paradox.

Install the point

Get the taper tool back out, and using the skinnier 5° blade, put a taper on the other end of the arrow. Heat the tip of the stick of ferrule cement over a candle until it's tacky like honey, then rub a dab onto the tapered tip of the shaft. Now grasp the point with your pliers, and heat it over the flame for about half a minute, turning it over from time to time so it heats evenly. Twist it onto the tapered shaft, with the heat from the point re-melting the ferrule cement. Turn the point a few times to get the ferrule cement well distributed. If the cement cools too fast, or you want to reposition the point, you can reheat the point in the candle as many times as you need to until you get it where you like it. When you're satisfied it's on straight, cool it in a cup of water. When it's cool enough to touch with your fingers, give it a firm twist to check if it's on tightly. If it's lose, reheat it and try again. You'd rather the point come off now in your hand than later in a target.

Fletch the arrow

The trick to fletching is that all three feathers must each go on exactly the same way, equally spaced, with the same twist, or else your arrow will not spin smoothly in flight. There are many different jigs designed to help with this, but the most common type has a chuck to hold the nock of

CRAFTS

the arrow, a fork to hold the shaft, and a big clip to hold a feather. The chuck can be rotated to lock into different angles, usually 120° increments. The clip that holds the feather against the arrow meets the shaft at a slight angle, so the feathers will cause the arrow to spin in flight, making it more stable. A *helical* clip will actually be warped as well, to increase this effect. If your clip is warped, it will be labeled for right-wing feathers or left-wing, and should be used with the appropriate type for the aerodynamics (arrow-dynamics?) to work out best.

Place your shaft in the jig, with the nock resting inside the chuck. We'll attach the cockfeather first, so rotate the chuck until the nock is perpendicular to the feather clip. If the nock is cockeyed in relation to the feather clip, then keep rotating the chuck until it clicks into the correct position; we'll use these other two positions later.

Take a feather, and place it into the clip so that the entire feather is covered and only the vein sticks out. Adjust the feather in the clip so that there is about an inch between the back of the feather and the

back of the clip; most clips have marks to help you get this consistent. If you don't leave enough space, your fletchings will be too far back on the arrow and your fingers will ruffle them when you draw the arrow. Now, place a thin bead of glue along the bottom of the vein, and slide the arrow clip into place on the jig, ensuring that there is good contact between the feather and the shaft along the entire length. Take a break for a few minutes.

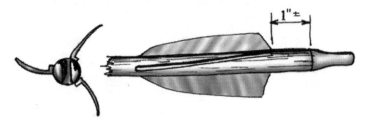

Once the glue has dried, open the feather clip and remove it from the jig. Rotate the chuck, locking it into the next position. Load another feather of a second color into the feather clip and glue it down as described before. Once that's dry, repeat the process with a third feather, also of the second color. Remove the arrow from the jig when everything is completely dry.

Finally, put a dab of glue over the front and back of each feather to help them stay on the shaft if the arrow passes all the way through a target butt.

Fletching tape is a relatively new product that can save a lot of time. It's basically a very narrow piece of tenacious double-sided tape that replace the fletching cement. Simply stick it to the vein of the feather, peel the backing off of the tape, and stick the feather to the shaft. No mess, no waiting.

Paint the crest

All that is left is painting the *crest,* those colored bands that identify the arrow's owner. This step is optional, but is good to do if you have the means, because it gives young archers another opportunity to personalize their tackle. Select a paint that is durable and waterproof, such as model enamel or acrylics. You can use a brush to apply it, but paint pens seem to work well and leave no mess. If your shaft is sealed, check to make sure the paint and sealer are compatible.

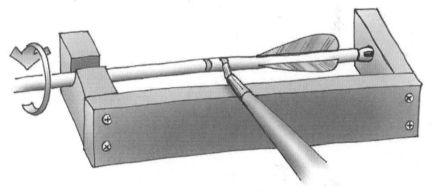

Perfect rings are best achieved by turning the arrow in a painting jig. You can buy motorized versions that spin the arrow automatically, but a more cost-effective solution is to make a simple jig yourself. The picture above shows a homemade jig consisting of two blocks of wood connected to a base, one with a groove for the shaft, and one with a shallow hole for the nock. To use it, lay your brush or paint pen gently against the shaft and rotate the arrow with your hand. A smooth band of color will appear around the shaft. By combining many rings of different colors and widths, an infinite range of crests can be invented, so you can tell the arrows of all your archers apart. Once the crest is thoroughly dry, it's a good idea to put a coat of clear varnish or sealer over it to keep it from getting worn off as it rubs against the arrow rest when shot.

CRAFTS

Every
English
archer
bears under
his girdle
24
Scots.

~ medieval proverb

Though it isn't necessary to know about the history of archery to use
a bow, an understanding of its origins helps to better your understanding
the craft. Spinning tales of archery lore is also a good way to entertain kids
between rounds of shooting, and gives them something to think about after
they leave the range. My hope is that by giving a fast and loose overview of
world archery history, some of these tales might interest you in learning
more. The internet and books from the local library will allow you to
expand your overall knowledge of archery's rich heritage, and you can pass
that along to your students.

Like much of history, the history of archery has been driven by
people: in some cases, it's an individual making a great accomplishment
or invention; in others, it's entire nations making war or changing public
policy. It's often difficult to tell if archery changes the course of history, or
the other way around. As Fred Bear said, "The history of the bow and arrow
is the history of mankind."

The Beginnings

Archery has been around since before recorded civilization. Through
archaeological evidence, we know that humans started using bows over
50,000 years ago. These earliest archers used arrows with heads of flint, a
technology that remained unchanged until relatively recently, within the
last few millennia. Some Native Americans were still using flint arrowheads
even into the beginning the 20th century[1].

Our knowledge of bow construction is less accurate, as the wood
and other organic materials used to make them are subject to decay.
Occasionally, however, fate preserves enough material to give archaeologist
a glimpse of ancient archery technology. In 1991, mountain climbers
discovered the frozen body of a prehistoric archer in a thawing glacier. Ötzi
(as he is now known) lived on the border between modern day Austria
and Italy in roughly 3300 BC, and carried with him the oldest surviving
examples of archery equipment that we have today. His tackle included
fourteen flint-headed arrows made from viburnum and dogwood, as well as
an unfinished yew longbow.

LORE

---

1. The Yahi of southern California were one example; you can read about them in *Ishi in
Two Worlds: A Biography of the Last Wild Indian in North America*, by Theodora Kroeber
(1961).

Only slightly less ancient are a group of bows found in bogs in northern Europe, where the cold brackish water has protected them from air, heat, and sunlight. These bows date from the second millennium B.C. and show that by this time man had already perfected several different styles of bow, from the paddle-limbed flatbow of Holmegaard in Denmark, to the D-sectioned longbow of Aschcott Heath in England.

Ancient Egypt

In more advanced cultures to the south, written records and paintings were better able to survive the ravages of time. Egyptians used archery as early as 5,000 BC, and by 2,000 BC had progressed to arrowheads made of hammered copper and bronze. Amenhotep II (ca.1428-1397 BC) was especially known for his archery prowess[2]. In one well-documented instance, this Egyptian pharaoh wielded a bow so powerful only he could draw it. While riding his chariot at full speed, he shot at four massive targets made from hammered copper as thick as a man's palm, piercing them each with his arrows. This display wasn't just idle bragging; he went on to lead his armies to victory in several wars where archery played a critical role.

Classical Greece

The early Greeks of the classical period used the bow, and knowledge of its use was considered important to any well-rounded noble. One of the most venerated deities of the Greek pantheon was Artemis, goddess of archery and the hunt. The bow and arrow figure prominently in Greek literature as well, such as the dramatic (if a bit gory) ending of Homer's Odyssey: after her husband Ulysses was thought lost at sea, many aggressive suitors pressured the lovely Penelope to remarry. She finally gave in to their nagging, and claimed that she would marry whichever one was strong enough to string her husband's bow. The suitors demanded that the mighty weapon be brought into the feasting hall. One by one, all of the suitors tried to string it and failed, until the challenge fell to a tired looking beggar at the end of the line. Unknown to them, the beggar was the disguised Ulysses himself, just returned from his adventures abroad. He was strong enough to string his own bow, of course, and repaid the suitors by shooting each of them full of arrows as they ran around screaming and trying to escape from the feast hall.

---

2.   Digital Egypt, http://www.digitalegypt.ucl.ac.uk/chronology/amenhotepii.html

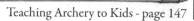

The Roman Empire

Archery continued to be practiced by the Romans, following in the tradition of the Greeks they so much admired. Even the Roman goddess Diana was an adaptation of the Greek Artemis, and continued to shoot arrows with deadly accuracy in their mythology as well. Although the armies of Rome were more famous for their use of spears, shields, and highly evolved tactical formations, archery was used as well. Several emperors were well known for their love of the bow, and Ascham mentions that "Domitian the Emperor was so cunning in shooting that he could shoot betwixt a man's fingers standing afar off, and never hurt him. Comodus also was excellent..."

Vikings and Scandinavia

The Vikings and other Scandinavian people of the 8th century knew archery, but it was used more as a hunting tool than a weapon of war. Perhaps these wild warriors from the north preferred the excitement of actually fighting their opponents hand-to-hand? Their bows were medium length self-bows, carved from a single piece of wood. Although they lacked the armor-penetrating power of later medieval bows, they would have been more than adequate for use against game animals or the occasional defenseless village.

The Golden Age of the Longbow

The English of the middle ages imported and perfected the Welsh yew longbow. These bows were about six feet long and had draw weights of from 100 to 150 pounds. The soldiers that trained to use them were required to practice every Sunday, and this became an after-church ritual. Skeletons of archers from the period have curved spines and other deformities from the massive muscles required to pull such powerful bows. During the 100 Years War with France, England used its archers to good effect several times. In the battles of Crécy (1346) and Poitiers (1356), English archers proved their worth by launching hundreds of thousands of arrows at French troops, killing about a hundred French soldiers for every English archer. Their bows were so strong that accounts form the period record archers shooting through two-inch-thick oak doors to get at enemies on the other side. The shooting style of these archers was different as well; the English longbowmen used only their index finger and middle finger when drawing.

LORE

Medieval Legends

It was during the troubled years of the early 13th century that archery's most famous legend, Robin Hood, evolved. Although opinion varies on exactly who he was and when he lived, many aspects of the legend are consistent throughout the tales. He and his band of "merry men" lived in Sherwood Forest in southern England, and spent their days hunting the king's deer, robbing the rich, helping the poor, and generally having a good time at the expense of the establishment. Robin Hood's skills with the longbow were unmatched by any man alive, and his daring acts of heroism leave such an impression on the listener that he's still remembered 800 years later.

About a hundred years after the bandit of Sherwood Forest, another famous archery hero turned up in Switzerland. Whereas Robin Hood was a charismatic leader of men, William Tell was a family man and an individualist. Legend has it that this skilled crossbowman was walking through the town square one morning, and he refused to kneel before the hat of a noble that had been placed upon a pole. The wicked noble took offense and had William Tell thrown in jail, threatening to keep him there forever unless he attempted a difficult task: Tell must shoot an apple off of his own son's head. He could not support his family while in jail, so Tell agreed. When the fateful day arrived, the entire town gathered to watch the shot. The son had so much faith in his father that he showed no fear, giving Tell confidence to take the shot, splitting the apple. Despite his confidence, he had hidden a second crossbow bolt in his shirt, with the intention of shooting the noble next if his son had died. News of this angered the noble, but Tell was able to escape his pursuers by fleeing into the countryside. The noble and his men pursued him for days, but he eventually secured his freedom permanently by ambushing them and shooting the noble through the heart. William Tell was never heard from again, though the Swiss are still inspired by him to this day for his stand against oppressive government.

Asiatic Archery of the Middle Ages

At about the same time on the other side of the planet, Genghis Khan and his horde of Mongols swept across Asia, using their combined archery and riding skills to defeat every army they met. Mongol archers wielded short, highly recurved composite bows made from horn and sinew capable of shooting 200 yards or more. This considerably outdistanced any other archers of the period. Their tactic was to ride to within range of the enemy and shoot arrows at them until the enemy got close enough to shoot back. Then, they would suddenly ride away. They repeated this until their enemies ran out of soldiers.

The Fall of Archery

With the advent of firearms in the 15th century, archery started to disappear as a tool of war. At first, guns were only superior because they required less training to use. But as technology progressed, they soon became faster to load, more accurate, and able to strike targets at greater distances than bows. It wasn't long before guns were adopted for hunting as well. One man attempted to singlehandedly hold off the inevitable victory of the gun: educator and writer Roger Ascham. In 1545, he published the first written treatise on teaching archery, *Toxophilus*. His book contained two parts: a section debating the merits of archery , and a section instructing the reader in the use of archery. Ascham was well respected as a teacher and thinker (he was Queen Elizabeth's personal childhood tutor), and his pro-archery politics were appreciated by the English king Henry VIII , himself a strong proponent of archery and a skilled bowman. Despite its popularity, however, this masterwork only postponed the inevitable demise of archery.

In the same year that Acham published *Toxophilus*, one of England's great warships, the *Mary Rose*, sank in the north Atlantic. This was an inconvenience to Henry VIII, but a blessing to archers and historians of the 20th century. The wreck was located and identified in the late 1960s, and in 1982 was raised by archaeologists and painstakingly examined. Within the wreck were numerous archery artifacts, including leather bracers, 137 longbows, and over 3500 arrows. Much of what we know today about late medieval archery comes from this treasure trove of archaeology, but mysteries remain: no bowstrings were recovered, and to this day no one can definitively say exactly how a medieval bowstring was made.

Archery Survives Elsewhere

In the closing years of the 16th century, the bow had all but disappeared, becoming a lawn game for the noble elite, much like tennis or croquet. In these dark years of European archery, the sport continued to survive in the Middle East in the form of *flight archery*. This was a competition purely for distance, and in Istanbul in 1798, Sultan Selim III set a distance record of 928 yards. Like those of the Mongols, Turkish bows were highly recurved and constructed from a composite of horn and sinew. These bows were drawn with the thumb rather than the fingers, because a shorter bow produces a sharper string angle at the nock of the arrow, pinching a three-fingered grip. A special thumb ring was used to ensure a crisp release.

LORE

Japanese Archery

In ancient Japan, a specialized form of archery called *kyudo* developed. The Japanese longbow is easily recognized because the upper limb is much longer than the lower limb, giving the bow a lopsided appearance. Skilled artisans make these bows from thin laminations of bamboo, a durable material readily available in Japan. Archery was considered a skill critical to a well-rounded samurai, and the art and philosophy of *kyudo* lives on to this day.

Yabusame is a centuries-old archery demonstration and ceremony that continues to be practiced in modern Japan, as well. This Shinto ceremony begins with prayer and peace offerings, and culminates with archers riding horses at full gallop while shooting *kaburaya* arrows at three square wooden targets. The earliest records of *yabusame* go back to the 6th century, and in the year 1096 it was performed in the presence of Emperor Shirakawa. If an archer were to miss a target in front of such an important audience, he was expected to commit suicide immediately.

Archery in the New World

The Incas, Aztecs, and other pre-Columbian cultures of the western hemisphere developed many advanced technologies, and archery was one of them. Since the dawn of man, archery in south and central America flourished and developed independently of the rest of the world[3]. In the

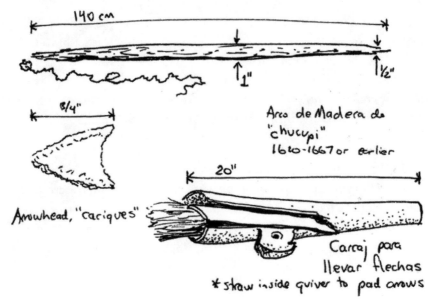

140 cm

1"   ½"

3/4"

Arco de Madera de "chucupi" 1610-1667 or earlier

20"

Arrowhead, "caciques"

Carcaj para llevar flechas

* straw inside quiver to pad arrows

---

3.   These sketches of ancient indigenous archery tackle were made by the author while in South America. They are a bow, arrowhead, and wooden quiver.

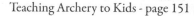

late 16th century, however, the Spanish conquistadores arrived and began a period of intense warfare and imperialism in the Western hemisphere. Many Spanish died at the hands of the skilled native archers during these early years of settlement, but the bow would eventually prove no match for the gun, for many of the reasons the Europeans had discovered a century before: a skilled archer required years of training, but a soldier could be trained to kill with a gun in a matter of days. The natives continued using archery for both hunting and warfare until many years into the Spanish incursion, but in the end, they could not replace their losses as quickly as the settlers, and South American archery disappeared forever.

Archery Rediscovered

Archery in western Europe remained in the shadows until the late 19th century, when it was resurrected for the masses as a tool for sport and pleasure. Although this resurgence began in Britain, it was felt more keenly in the United States when Maurice Thompson published *The Witchery of Archery*, igniting the passion of a new generation of archers. He and other Confederate soldiers returned from the Civil War to find food scarce, money tight, game plentiful, and guns outlawed. The bow was an ideal solution to their dilemma.

Native Americans relied on archery as a means to acquire food for thousands of years. Their legacy was nearly lost in the late 1800s as tribes were forced off of their land and moved to reservations, disrupting their traditional way of life- including archery. But in a twist of fate, a man named Ishi was discovered in 1911 in the countryside near Oroville, California. He was nearly starved, dressed in tatters, and spoke no English. At first he was thought to be insane and placed in a jail, but it was soon discovered that he was actually the last surviving member of the Yahi tribe of Native Americans. He spent the remaining five years of his life working with anthropologists and archers, teaching modern Americans how the ancient natives had lived. He met several famous archers and bowyers of the time including Dr. Saxton Pope, and taught them many forgotten secrets of the art of archery.

Archery Gains Popularity

The early 20th century saw archery in North America develop fully into what it is today. Several famous archers rose to prominence in these years.

Dr. Saxton Pope (1875-1926) and Art Young (1883-1935) were pioneers in the use of archery as a sport. Renaissance men, Pope and Young were archers, bowyers, sportsman, adventurers, writers, and big game hunters. They hunted bear in Alaska, lions in Africa, and just about everything in between. They invented modern broadhead designs and pioneered new bow styles. They experimented with what archery could do, and pushed the conceptual boundaries of what the sport was about. But most importantly, they recorded their journeys in books and journal publications, so that an entire generation of would-be archers could benefit from their learning.

Howard Hill (1900-1975) is often called "the greatest archer that ever lived". Whereas Pope & Young helped archers everywhere advance the craft, Howard Hill brought archery to the non-shooting masses. He was big, friendly, outgoing, and extremely entertaining. His prowess with the bow was legendary, as was his popularity. In 1941, he drew a crowd of 30,000 people to a stadium in Chicago just to see him shoot. He was also a Hollywood personality; his amazing archery shots can be seen to this day in *The Adventures of Robin Hood* with Errol Flynn. In an age before special effects, every arrow shot in that film comes from Hill's bow off-screen, streaking across the scenery and plunking into a stuntman hiding a three inch thick piece of balsa wood under his shirt. He even shot an apple off of the head of a stuntman from 60 yards away. A big game hunter as well, Hill is noted as being the first white man to kill an elephant with the bow and arrow- a feat he did with a 115-pound bow and a 41-inch arrow.

The Boy Scouts of America has supported archery in their program since its beginnings in 1911. The Archery merit badge is one of the more challenging to this day, requiring minimum scores in several different types of rounds. But even the Boy Scouts' take on archery has evolved over the years, and most archers of today would be hard pressed to complete some of the requirements of the original Archery merit badge of 1911. These included things like making a bow and arrow from scratch that are capable of shooting effectively to a hundred feet, or being able to shoot so far and fast as to have six arrows in the air at once.

Modern Archery

As the 20th century progressed, many technical innovations in archery equipment were made possible by advances in engineering and materials. Fiberglass and flat-limbed recurve technology evolved in the late '30s, and Doug Easton began mass producing aluminum arrows in the '40s, setting a new benchmark for arrow uniformity and reliability. In the '50s, plastic vanes became available, and in the late '60s, the Wilbur Allen invented the

compound bow, changing archery forever. By the early '90s, bows could be fitted with Kevlar strings, laser sights, magnesium risers, and carbon fiber arrows. In the 21st century, keeping abreast of the current archery technology is as much of a challenge as actually using it.

Today, archery continues to thrive along three major lines, the largest of which is bowhunting. A century ago, this activity was reserved for the eccentric and relatively wealthy, but today bowhunting is popular all over the country. Game such as deer or turkey is commonly taken by bow, with the archers enjoying special advantages over gun-toting hunters, like extended seasons and larger bag limits. Bowhunters feel that the skill required to hunt this way is more challenging, the equipment brings them closer to nature, and it is more humane than hunting with a gun because an archer must make a more considered shot (making a non-lethal wound less likely). Fred Bear (1902-1988), one of modern bowhunting's biggest proponents, helped bring new innovations like fiberglass composite bows and compound bows to the mass market. Bowhunting equipment is the bread-and-butter business from which most archery equipment manufacturers make their living.

A smaller branch of modern archery is target shooting. This takes many forms, from friendly target shooting and archery class at summer camp, to the competitive ranges of tournament and Olympic archery. People all over are enjoying archery; it's affordable, healthy, relaxing, and accessible to everyone.

We bring this story full circle with the third branch of modern archery: traditional archery. Some traditional archers enjoy the simplicity of making and shooting primitive gear; others combine archery with historical reenactment. Groups such as the Society for Creative Anachronism sponsor historically inspired tournaments and shoots, challenging archers to use period equipment and often banning modern conveniences such as sights, compound bows, fiberglass, and aluminum. The British Long-Bow Society sponsors special tournaments for traditional longbow shooters, using a "standard arrow" patterned after historical military examples from the golden age of English archery. These monster projectiles measure at least 3/8" diameter, 32" long, and weight 800 grains or more in weight!

Now, let's look at a few of the people that made archery what it is today.

LORE

Maurice Thompson (1844~1901)

The Witchery of Archery was the main inspiration for the increase of interest in archery in the United States at the beginning of this century. Dr. R. P. Elmer wrote of it, 'That wonderful little book has as much effect on archery as Uncle Tom's Cabin had on the civil war!'
 -Joe St. Charles, from the preface to the second edition of
 The Witchery of Archery (1879)

Maurice (pronounced "Morris") Thompson had the misfortune of being born into a troubled time in America. The mid-1800s were filled with conflict over slavery and state sovereignty, culminating in the Civil War in 1861. He was a 17 year old Georgian at the time, and was soon drawn into the conflict on the side of the Confederate Army. He served as a scout and soldier, and by combining his knowledge of the forest with a little bit of luck, survived the deadliest war in American history.

Upon returning to Georgia, he found that his family's home had been burned to the ground by Union troops. He tried to make a living doing odd jobs and hunting for squirrels to fill his plate, but he soon realized that the ruinous postwar economy of the South left him little opportunity. He spent evenings studying law books by firelight, and soon moved north to Crawfordsville, Indiana.

During the years immediately following the war, Southerners weren't allowed to possess guns, so Maurice and his brother Will returned to their friend from childhood, the bow. Maurice hunted small game to feed his family, and occasionally returned to the South to visit the land of his forefathers and perfect his archery skills.

Archery soon became his passion. He began a law practice in Crawfordsville, but spent all of his spare time shooting, either in the fields at game, or in the archery club he started, the Wabash Merry Bowmen. Others soon discovered archery with him, and the club grew. In 1878, Maurice Thompson published *The Witchery of Archery*, a slim book credited with instigating the rebirth of archery in America. It sold out quickly, and was reprinted in 1879 to fill the demands of eager archers. For centuries before, archery had only been a lawn game for the aristocratic elite, but now it was finding its way into the lives of the everyday farmers and workers.

Maurice wrote about some of the technical aspects of archery, but his true talent was describing the sights and sounds of the woods from the viewpoint of the archer. His love for the earth and its creatures is apparent in his prose, and the reader can truly believe that he was never happier than when standing in a quiet forest with bow in hand.

With the increase in the popularity of archery, the National Archery Association was formed in 1879. Its first meeting was in Crawfordsville, Indiana and Maurice Thompson was elected the first Chairman. With the success of *The Witchery of Archery* and other writings, Maurice was able to leave his law practice and write full-time about archery, the outdoors, and related subjects. Because of his eloquence, vision, and passion, he became known as the father of American archery.

Though he lived in a time filled with Victorian ideas, he was at times somewhat progressive in his thinking. He touted archery as good exercise, which he felt to be essential to well being. Even women could benefit from the sport, as he mentions in *The Witchery of Archery*:

"Social science begins with physical culture. The world must be moved by muscle as well as mind. The nearer women approach to the standard of the physical power possessed by men, the nearer they will be able to make their mental prowess recognized by the world.... Women who are agitating the question of women's enfranchisement must learn that "might makes right" is not a maxim of immortality when clearly understood... Men and women must be borne together to the high plane of the millennium, and none but perfectly developed bodies and souls can bear the strain of the lifting."

Further Reading

You can read about many of his archery adventures in his landmark book, *The Witchery of Archery*. As it says in the preface, "Maurice Thompson's expertise as a writer, combined with a strong love for the sport, makes this book still one of the finest ever written on sylvan archery."

LORE

Ishi (1862?–1916)

On the morning of August 29, 1911, a man was discovered cornered by dogs in a stockyard near Oroville, California. He was nearly starved, dressed in tatters, and spoke no English. The locals first thought him insane and placed him in a jail, but it was soon discovered that he was actually the last surviving member of the Yahi tribe of Native Americans. Word of this amazing find soon spread, drawing gawkers and onlookers from far and wide. A pair of anthropologists from the University of California in San Francisco, professors Kroeber and Waterman, appeared several days later. Using hand gestures and pieces of various ancient Indian dialects from their studies, they were able to roughly communicate with Ishi (pronounced ee-shee[1]) and offered to take him with them to San Francisco. He accepted.

Upon arriving in the big city, Ishi began the process of adapting to the alien ways of the white man: dress clothes, streetcars, artificial lighting, and money were all new concepts to him. Kroeber and Waterman took good care of Ishi, though, watching out for his well being and fending off circus recruiters and newspapermen who would take advantage of him. They gave him a job as a live-in janitor in the University of California's anthropological museum, as a way to legitimize the support Ishi was receiving from the university. Ishi, being a noble sort, would not accept charity unless he could do something in return, so the museum set up a "living exhibit", much like in a zoo. For several hours a day, Ishi would live in this artificial environment, making stone tools, leather clothing, bows, and arrows while being observed by museum patrons and researchers.

Ishi realized that his old life would never return, so he devoted himself to mastering his new surroundings. He continued to improve his English and learn the ways of the white man. It was at about this time that he met Dr. Saxton Pope, a physician who was invited to perform Ishi's general health checkups. Dr. Pope was quite interested in archery, and the two became friends almost immediately and remained close for the rest of Ishi's life. They would spend afternoons together shooting archery and discussing technique. Ishi knew many secrets of bow and arrow construction long thought forgotten, and he shared them with his friend Pope, who in turn wrote about them in his books, returning this ancient knowledge back to society.

Dr. Pope noted several peculiarities of Ishi's archery style. Unlike most archers, Ishi placed the arrow on the far side of his bow, and rested the

---

1. According to his friend Saxton Pope (*Hunting with the Bow and Arrow*, p. 5)

shaft on an extended finger, rather than the knuckle or top of the fist. His grip was unique, as well: he drew the string with his thumb much like the ancient Turks and Mongols of central Asia. But unlike the Turks, he used no thumb ring and locked his thumb lightly with the tip of his middle finger. This leads to some speculation about a connection between the earliest Americans migrating across the Bering land bridge and bringing this style of shooting with them, but it is equally likely that this style could have developed in more than one place simultaneously, as good ideas often do.

Ishi always shot from a crouching position, reaching across his body with the bow held at a diagonal to remain clear of the ground. This was because archery was his tool for hunting, and this position offered the best concealment from game. Pope noted that even though Ishi's favorite bows drew only 40 pounds at 25 inches, his marksmanship was excellent and he never had any difficulty killing his prey. He held his bow lightly, as well, and when he shot it turned over slowly in his hand much as you would see when watching modern Olympic archers.

Ishi also showed Pope his techniques for making bows and arrows. A bow was made from juniper and other indigenous woods, and its width and length were based on specific proportions that related to the person Ishi was making it for. Arrows were made from hazel or some other straight wood, and he built them in groups of five, because five was a sacred number to his people. His arrowheads were of chipped flint. Making equipment was a ceremonial as well as funtional activity.

Ishi died on March 25, 1916 from tuberculosis and related complications, after spending only five years in modern society. He was estimated to be in his mid fifties; though he led an active, healthy lifestyle, his body did not have well developed defenses against the foreign diseases of the white man.

Further Reading

For further information on the life of Ishi, I recommend *Ishi in Two Worlds: A Biography of the Last Wild Indian in North America*, by Theodora Kroeber. A shorter history of Ishi specific to his archery can be found in the first chapters of *Hunting with the Bow and Arrow*, by his friend and fellow archer Saxton Pope.

LORE

Pope, Young, & Compton (1863-1938)

*The flight of the arrow is symbolic of life itself. It springs : om the bow
with high aim, flies towards the blue heaven above, and seems to have
immortal power. The song if its life is sweet to the ear. The rush of its
upward arc is a promise of perpetual progress. With perfect grace it
sweeps onward, though less aspiring. Then fluttering imperceptibly, it
points downward and with ever-increasing speed, approaches the earth,
where, with a deep sigh, it sinks in the soil, quivers with spent energy,
and capitulates to the inevitable.*

Thus writes Saxton Pope, in his book *Hunting with the Bow and Arrow,*
first published in 1923. A twisted trail led Saxton Pope to archery. He
mentions playing with bows and arrows in his youth, hiding in the hills and
pretending to be Robin Hood, but he never seriously pursued the craft until
he met Ishi, the last of the Yahi tribe. Dr. Pope was teaching surgery at the
University Medical School in San Francisco at the time, and was asked to be
Ishi's personal physician. Their relationship was as first formal, but as they
got to know each other, they developed a strong friendship. In the few years
before Ishi's death from tuberculosis, Pope became immersed in archery
and learned many of the ancient unrecorded secrets of Yahi bowmaking and
archery.

Also during these brief years with Ishi, many archery enthusiasts
were drawn to San Francisco to meet the famous Indian archer, and by
coincidence met Saxton Pope as well. Among these were Art Young, a
strong young newspaperman, and Will Compton, a recently unemployed
bowyer. After Ishi's passing, their friendship was tightened and "then our
serious work began," as Pope says.

The trio spent countless hours hunting in the scrublands of California
and pursuing practical research on archery sciences like bow wood
properties, effectiveness of arrowhead types, and methods of shooting. They
honed their skills and chased increasingly larger game. This was a time when
archery was uncommon, and most gun-carrying hunters they met derided
them as foolhardy, sure that their flimsy bows would be unable to kill "real"
game animals.

These taunts only solidified their determination, and over the next few
decades they set out to prove that the longbow was a potent tool for taking
game of any type. They started with rabbits and deer, working their way up
to bobcat and black bear. Eventually, the California Academy of Sciences
commissioned them to kill several grizzlies for a museum display in Golden

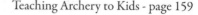

Gate Park. Although they had several near-death experiences, they were successful in bringing back many grizzly specimens, including an enormous 1,000 pound grizzly that Art Young killed with a single arrow. They continued to expand the boundaries of what was thought possible with the bow and arrow, eventually delving into Africa to hunt lions and other safari animals.

Pope, Young, and Compton were true renaissance men, well-rounded in a wide range of pursuits besides archery. Pope played the mandolin and Young the violin, and they often took these into the field, playing duets by the evening campfire to while away the hours. Pope was a scholar and surgeon, and well known for his impromptu performances of sleight-of-hand magic tricks. Young was a newspaperman among other things, and both of them were excellent writers. Compton was a skilled bowyer and woodsman. He grew up amongst Sioux Indians, and was so knowledgeable about their ways that he had been adopted into the tribe.

These men made their own gear, a novel thing in those days. They did this in part out of necessity, as quality gear was often unavailable; but mostly they did it because they loved archery and all that goes with it. Compton worked for 19 years as a bowyer in Oregon before meeting the other two, and taught them much of what he knew of the craft. Pope's experiences with Ishi were also instrumental in their development of (what was at the time) modern archery equipment.

Although these three men were each a decade apart in age, they had a strong friendship and sense of adventure, and worked well as a team. Of the three, Art Young was considered to be the most athletic and the best shot. The older Will Compton had a great store of wisdom in woodcraft, stalking, and bowmaking; he was largely responsible for teaching the others how to make their equipment. Saxton Pope's intelligence, organization, and social connections made the logistics of their expeditions possible, as well as providing us with a written record of what happened.

Pope was the middle in age, but he died first in 1926 from pneumonia after returning from their African safari. A few years later in 1935 Art Young died from a ruptured appendix,. Will Compton died soon thereafter. It is a testament to their skill as outdoorsmen that they avoided death at the claws of grizzlies and lions.

LORE

History- Howard Hill (1900-1975)

Howard Hill was born on November 13, 1900 in Shelby County, Alabama. He began shooting the bow when only four years old, and was quite skilled with it by the time he want away to college. Although he excelled at many different physical activities such as baseball, basketball, and football, his true passion was archery. Aided by his powerful physique, he favored a bow that pulled from 80 to 90 pounds[1]. For many years, he held the record for the heaviest bow ever pulled, at 172 pounds, and he continued to pull bows up to 75 pound with ease well into his sixties.

His flexibility with all types of archery was astounding: in 1928 alone, he set a record for flight archery with a shot of 391 yards, won the Florida state target archery tournament, and won the first of seven archery golf tournaments (using the rules he himself had invented). After that, Hill went on to win 196 field archery tournaments in a row. Not content to stop there, he invented other more unusual forms of archery, such as underwater archery using custom-designed arrows and breathing equipment.

People began to call him "The World's Greatest Archer", and he appeared in three different World's Fairs to show his archery prowess that included feats like shooting tossed coins and aspirins out of the air. He toured the country, putting on demonstrations for schools and engaging in all things archery-related. In 1941, he performed in front of a crowd of 35,000 spectators who were so enthusiastic to see him that they tore away pieces of his clothing as souvenirs.

His skill with the bow combined with his natural friendliness also made him friends in the movie industry. He worked on several films, as a technical archery advisor and stunt shooter. In Errol Flynn's *The Adventures of Robin Hood* (1938), he performed amazing shots for the camera crew that would have been impossible with the special effect technology of the day, including a dramatic sequence where a soldier runs onscreen and is struck in the chest with an arrow- an arrow actually shot by Hill into a special wood and steel pad worn under the actor's shirt. During *The Adventures of Robin Hood*, he became friends with Flynn and went with him on various adventures, including a voyage on Flynn's yacht off the western coast of Mexico.

In his 1953 book *Hunting the Hard Way*, Hill describes many of his outrageous archery exploits. He hunted animals of all sorts, from large animals like moose, elk, and bighorn sheep to dangerous animals like bear, boar, and jaguar. When he'd killed everything available in the Americas,

---

1. Info from Howard Hill Archery, www.howardhillarchery.com

he toured Africa, hunting exotic beasts such as like lions, crocodiles, and zebra. In 1950, he became the first archer to kill an elephant without using a poisoned arrow[2]. To keep it interesting, he often experimented with alien surroundings: he shot a running bison while riding an Indian pony bareback, a swordfish from the deck of a sailboat, and a shark (it escaped) while underwater. Records show that he killed well over 2,000 animals in the fifty years he hunted.

A man of many talents, Hill also made his own bows, arrows, and other archery tackle. The company he started in the 1950s, Howard Hill Archery, is still in business today and makes custom longbows and equipment for traditional archers.

Despite the impressiveness of this list of accomplishments and awards, it doesn't well illustrate some of his best qualities. Howard Hill was a loving husband, and regularly took his wife with him on his outings and hunts (she was an accomplished archer and huntress in her own right). In a time when racism was rife in America, he developed close personal bonds with Native Americans like Charlie Snow, Mike Osceola, and others. He respected their heritage and skill with a bow. His native friends taught him an appreciation of nature and the environment, and he passed that appreciation along in his books, years before the naturalist agenda became mainstream.

Further Reading

To better understand man behind the statistics, I recommend his first (somewhat autobiographical) book, *Hunting the Hard Way*.

LORE

---

2. *Hunting the Hard Way* (1953)

50,000 bc	Date of oldest flint arrowheads discovered in Africa
8,000 bc	Simple self-bows used in Denmark
5,000 bc	Egyptian use of bow recorded
3,300 bc	"Ötzi", a Neolithic archer, dies in the Alps
2,800 bc	Composite bow first appears in Egypt
2,600 bc	Flatbows and longbows used in northern Europe
2,000 bc	Egyptians start using metal arrowheads of hammered copper
1,209 bc	Pharaoh Merneptah of Egypt's archers defeat Libyan army
250 bc	Parthians make effective use of cavalry archers
288	St. Sebastian martyred (patron saint of archers)
434	Atilla the Hun assumes leadership of Hungarian empire
552	Battle of Taginae, Roman archers defeat the Goths
1066	Battle of Hastings; King Harold killed by an arrow
1208	Genghis Khan assumes leadership of the Mongols
1200s	The legend of Robin Hood
1307	The legend of William Tell
1346	Battle of Crécy- English archers defeat French
1415	Battle of Agincourt- English archers defeat French, again
1457	Football and golf banned in England, as they interfere with archery practice
1477	Cricket banned in England, as it interferes with archery practice

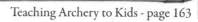

1508	Crossbow banned in England, as it interferes with archery practice
1545	Roger Ascham publishes *Toxophilus*
1545	The *Mary Rose* sinks near Portsmouth, England
1583	First recorded organized archery competition in Finsbury, England
1618-1648	Thirty Years' War, gunpowder replaces archery as the preferred tool of war
1644	Battle of Tipper Muir, last English archers used in war
1781	Toxophilite Society formed in England
1798	Sultan Selim shoots an arrow a record 972 yards
1806	Bowmaker Thomas Waring the Elder dies. His son continues the business.
1859	Horace Ford publishes *Archery, Its Theory and Practice*
1861	G.N.A.S. established in Liverpool, England
1878	Maurice Thompson publishes *The Witchery of Archery*
1879	National Archery Association established in Crawfordsville, Indiana
1900	Archery first appears as an Olympic sport
1911	Ishi emerges from the wilderness in California
1923	Saxton Pope publishes *Hunting with the Bow and Arrow*
1927	Abner Shepardson invents the first rudimentary bow sight
1931	F.I.T.A. established in Lwow, Poland
1930s	Flat-limbed recurves designed by engineers Hickman & Klopsted
1939	Doug Easton manufactures the first aluminum arrow
1951	Max Hamilton develops the first plastic vanes
1953	Howard Hill publishes *Hunting the Hard Way*
1969	Wilbur Allen invents the compound bow
1972	Archery returns to the Olympics after a 52-year absence
1983	First production carbon arrow, again by Easton

LORE

Besides being a healthy sport and an opportunity to learn history, archery is also a good place to demonstrate and discuss physics.

ARCHER'S PARADOX

Unless you are using a modern bow with a shoot-through riser, the width of your bow will cause the arrow to be pointed off-center in respect to the path of the bowstring. Luckily, you can still hit where you're aiming due to a peculiar phenomenon called *archer's paradox*[1].

When an archer releases an arrow, several forces act upon it and affect its flight. The string moves forward, pushing the arrow from behind. At the same time, the inertia of the arrowhead resists the forward motion, so the arrow becomes slightly compressed along its length. Because it is so thin and long, for a brief instant the arrow actually bends slightly instead of becoming imperceptibly shorter. The direction of the bend is away from the bow– in the case of a right handed archer, the middle of the arrow bends outward to the left. The amount of the bend is relative to the stiffness of the arrow; a stiffer arrow bends less than a more flexible arrow.

As you may remember, spine weight is actually a measure of an arrow's stiffness. An arrow with a spine properly matched to the bow will bend just enough so that its course will change towards the center of the target, balancing out the misalignment caused by the width of the bow. By the time the arrow is downrange, it's flying straight towards the target because the fletchings have enough air passing over them that they can stabilize the arrow aerodynamically.

If the arrow is not properly matched to the bow, problems ensue. An arrow that is too stiff for the bow will not bend enough to compensate for the misalignment caused by the bow, and will land to the left of where it's aimed (for a right-handed archer). Similarly, an arrow that is not stiff enough will bend too much, wrapping around the bow too much and landing to the right of the target.

Since arrows are grouped into five-pound spine weights, a picky archer will want to know how to fine-tune the arrows' spine weight to match the bow exactly. Making an arrow stiffer or flimsier is really not feasible, but there are two other ways to make an arrow bend more (or less). One way is to make the arrow shorter. A shorter arrow bends less when under the same stress as a longer one[2]; so by shortening an arrow you can make it

---

1. This phrase was originally used by Robert Elmer in the 1930s.
2. You can test this yourself: get a yardstick, put it between two tables 30 inches apart, and suspend a weight form the middle. Now, move the tables closer together, and notice how the yardstick bends less.

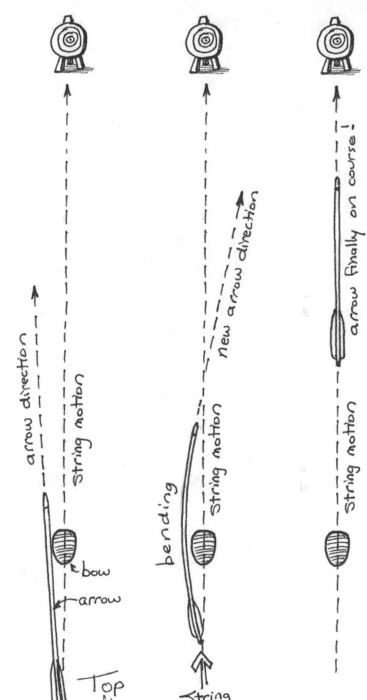

stiffer and get it to land farther to the left.

A second way to adjust an arrow's stiffness is to change the weight of the arrowhead. A heavier arrowhead has greater inertia to resist the string's motion, and will cause the arrow to bend more when the string is released. So, you could change to a heavier arrowhead to make your shots land farther right, or use a lighter one to get them to land farther left. Be advised, however, that changing the weight of your arrowheads will create as many problems as it solves, because lighter arrows have less time to be affected by gravity during their flight and will land higher up in the target than heavier ones.

For most archers having trouble finding the bull, the real culprits are shooting skills like aiming, anchor point, and release. Fine tuning arrow spine is more for archers who have high precision and consistently shoot slightly left or right of target when properly aiming at the center.

PAPER TUNING

Assuming proper technique by the archer, a well-tuned arrow will stabilize in flight and fly straight and true after only a few feet. Large oscillations, wiggling, or arrows landing crooked in the target are usually caused by archer error. However, small, consistent errors can be caused by subtle problems with the bow or arrow. You can easily make a simple apparatus to identify these fine tuning errors. Tape a large piece of lightweight paper tightly in a rigid frame of some sort, such as an old picture

frame or a square of lumber. Place it downrange about ten feet away form the archer, in the direction of the target. Shoot into the target as you normally would, so the arrow passes through the paper. By looking at the shape of the tear in the paper, you can figure out which way your arrow is turning in flight. If the hole is a circle with three notches (caused by the fletchings), then your arrow is already flying straight.

However, if the tear shows the fletching passing through the paper left or right of the shaft (such as in the picture to the right), then your spine weight is not exactly right for your bow. For a right-handed archer, if your fletchings are tearing the paper left of the shaft, then your arrow is too flexible and you need a stiffer arrow with a higher spine weight. If your fletchings are hitting too far right, the opposite

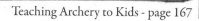

is true. For large errors, you should consider changing to the next higher or lower spine weight group, regardless of what your bow weight is. For small adjustments, consider changing arrow length or arrowhead weight as previously described.

If the tears in the paper are showing the fletchings striking high or low, then you probably have your nocking point in the wrong place. A high fletching (as seen at the left) indicates a too-high nocking point, and a vice-versa. Be careful, though; if you move the nocking point down to fix a too-high fletching, it's possible to move it so far down that the back of the arrow will bang off of the rest and kick upward, making it appear that your nocking point is too high.

If your error is diagonal, then you have two problems at once. Tackle them one at a time. The nocking point is the easiest to fix, so try that first; then tweak the arrow spine until you have them both sorted out and the arrow passes straight through the paper.

BASIC BALLISTICS

When a projectile (such as an arrow) travels through the air towards the target, it has two different forces opposing its effort: gravity, and drag[3]. Gravity is a natural downward force that holds us to the earth, and it affects everything including arrows. It is most easily understood as accelerating objects downward at about 32 feet per second per second. In the case of our arrow, if we dropped it from shoulder height (say, five feet) it would start with a speed of zero, and after a second, it would already be falling at a speed of 32 feet per second, and would continue accelerating from there. Obviously, it would hit the ground way before a second passed; we can skip any tricky math and say it would take about a quarter-second to hit the ground. If the arrow is moving forward (such as when shot from a bow), it will still take just as long to fall to the earth, but will also cover a lot of

---

3.   This overview of ballistics is a gross simplification of a science that engineers and mathematicians spent a few hundred years refining during the Enlightenment. Much more thorough information is available in the library or online, if you are interested.

LORE

horizontal distance during that same time. In this way, gravity essentially puts a limit on how far you can shoot. Higher arrow speeds allow you to send your arrow farther horizontally before it gets to the ground.

Drag is the second force acting against your arrow. As it moves forward, your arrow must push its way through the air, much like a canoe through the water. Air pushing back against the front of the arrow and pulling on the fletchings causes the arrow to go slower and slower. Realistically, your arrow will never quite stop, because it will contact the ground or target long before drag has such a drastic effect. Drag is a critical factor in arrow trajectory, though, because as it slows the arrow down, it gives gravity more of an opportunity to pull the arrow towards the earth. Gravity and drag are partners in a conspiracy to keep your arrow out of the target.

All of this is assuming that you are aiming the arrow at the horizon. In actuality, this rarely occurs. By aiming your arrow upwards, some of the arrow's forward energy is used to carry it upward a bit (called a "vertical vector" for you physics people), buying the arrow more time to get some horizontal distance covered before gravity finally wins again. The more you increase your upward aim, the more it increases your vertical vector, which increases your time aloft, which increases your overall distance.

There is a point, however, at which aiming at a higher trajectory no longer gets you more distance. This is usually around 45 degrees to the horizon. Above this angle, so much of the arrow's energy is spent going up and down that relatively little is left to do the horizontal movement. An extreme example of this is if you shoot straight up: ALL of the energy is spent on vertical movement, and no horizontal travel happens at all[4].

The only other ballistics item really worth mentioning is *point blank range*. This is the magical place at which, for a given distance, the upward angle of your shot gives your arrow exactly enough upward energy so it will travel up and down in the same amount of time it takes it to cover the horizontal distance to the target. Or to put it another way, the arrow lands exactly where you aimed it; no higher, no lower.

---

4.   Look out! Incoming arrow!

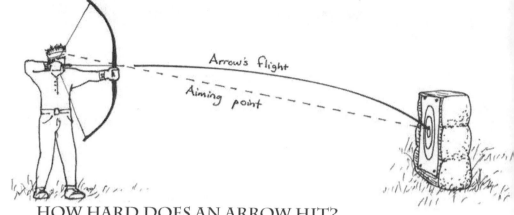

Arrow's flight

Aiming point

HOW HARD DOES AN ARROW HIT?

Generally, the impact force an arrow delivers to a target only concerns a narrow group of archers. Bowhunters care, because more force means better penetration and greater injury to their quarry. Medieval soldiers cared for the same reason, but also because an arrow with little power would be ineffective against armor. A forceful shot has usefulness even in certain target shooting situations, like the Cherokee cornstalk shoot. So, what variables affect the hitting force of an arrow?

Physicists think of this as "kinetic energy," and it can be described by the following equation:

$$E_k = \tfrac{1}{2}\, mv^2$$

where E_k is kinetic energy
m= mass of the arrow
v= velocity of the arrow

Finding an actual numeric value for the energy of your arrow is not very useful; for most archers it's more important to understand that the only two factors affecting an arrow's energy are the mass and velocity of the arrow[5]. In a practical sense, that means that making the arrow travel faster is much more effective for increasing its force than adding weight. This further reinforces that idea faster is better; in addition to dropping less due to gravity, a faster arrow also has much more force than a heavy arrow.

LORE

---

5.   Notice as well that bow weight and size have no direct effect on arrow energy.

The modern hunting gun
is an irresistable
weapon of wholesale murder;
and is just as deadly no matter
who pulls the trigger. It
spreads terror as well as death
by its loud discharge, and
leaves little clue as to who
is responsible for the shot...
the bow is a far less
destructive weapon, and to
succeed at all in the chase,
the bowman must be a
double-read forester.

-Handbook for Boys, 1911
Boy Scouts of America

Archery, being an ancient and specialized sport, has a vocabulary all its own. Some words in this glossary are so old that they have fallen into general disuse, but will still crop up from time to time. Others are so specific or specialized that you will only hear them in the context of archery.

3D targets: Freestanding targets that can be shot from any angle. Usually made of foam and shaped like animals, such as deer or turkeys.

accuracy: The closeness of an archer's shot to the center of the target. Not to be confused with *precision*.

Agincourt, Battle of (1415 AD): Historical event in which English archers massacred thousands of highly trained, well equipped French knights while only losing a few hundred men themselves.

aluminum: a strong, lightweight metal used for making arrows and sometimes bows.

AMO: Archery Manufacturing Organization, a group that established archery equipment standards.

AMO length: The length of a bow string based on the AMO's measuring procedure; it generally works out to be four inches longer than the actual string length.

anchor point: The position of the archer's drawing hand at full draw.

archer: Someone engaging in the ancient and honorable art of shooting a bow.

archer's paradox: The phenomenon where an arrow bends around the bow after release, then springs back to shape and oscillates during flight.

arm guard: See *bracer*.

arrow: A straight, thin projectile shot from a bow.

arrowhead: The forward most part of the arrow; it comes in many types and shapes.

arrowsmith: A person who makes arrowheads (not to be confused with a *fletcher*, see below).

artillery shooting: Another name for *roving mark*.

back: The side of the bow that faces away from the archer when held in the shooting position.

backstop: Something behind the target to keep stray arrows from leaving the range.

barb: A rearward facing spike or hook on an arrowhead to prevent it from being easily removed. Common on fishing arrows; often illegal on hunting arrows.

barred: Feather fletchings that still show the original markings of the turkey.

barreled: An arrow shaft that is wider at the center than the ends.

barebow shooting: Shooting without the use of a mechanical sight.

bastard string: A longer string that is used to temporarily pull a compound bow far enough to attach the main string.

belly: The side of the bow that faces towards the archer when held in the shooting position.

Beursault: A traditional French archery shoot down a narrow alleyway. See the section on Activities for a lengthier description.

bionic deer: A steel, deer-shaped 3D target with a tiny foam insert in the vital area, so that all less-than-perfect shots will result in broken arrows.

blunt: A type of arrowhead that is flat or rounded, and designed not to penetrate the target.

bobtailed: An arrow shaft that is tapered towards the fletchings.

bodkin: A type of arrowhead that is narrow, pyramidal, and edgeless. It was historically used in times of war for piercing armor, and is rarely used in contemporary archery.

boss: a large round disc-shaped target, usually made from woven rye straw, covered with fabric, and supported on a tripod.

bow: In its simplest form, a piece of wood with a string that is strained to shoot an arrow.

bowhunting: Using a bow to kill an animal. It requires special licensure, equipment, and training that is beyond the scope of this text.

bowfishing: Using a bow to shoot fish. Legal only for certain types of fish, it requires special licensure, equipment, and training that is beyond the scope of this text.

bowstring: The string that bends the bow and launches the arrow.

bowstave: The actual bow itself, without the string. It's a somewhat archaic term.

bowyer: A person who makes bows.

bow press: A clamping device used to hold bows for tuning and stringing, usually for compound bows

bow reel: A fishing reel that mounts on the front of a bow for bowfishing.

bow square: A "T"-shaped tool for accurately locating the nocking point.

bow stringer: A cord with a small pocket on each end, used to aid the archer in stringing the bow.

brace (v): An old expression, meaning to string the bow.

brace height: See *fistmele*

bracer: A protective pad or wrap for the archer's forearm, to protect against string slap.

broadhead: A type of arrowhead that is triangular when viewed from the side, with two or more razor edges. Used for hunting.

bull: The gold center of the target face, also called the *bullseye*.

butt: The large mass behind the target face that the arrow sticks into, often made of hay, straw, excelsior, or sisal. In older contexts, it is a mound of dirt.

cam: An asymmetrical wheel on a compound bow. The shape of the cam controls letoff.

cable: The metal "strings" in a compound bow that crisscross over the cams and pulleys.

carriage bow: An older term for a *take-down bow*.

cement: Adhesive (see also *fletching cement* & *ferrule cement*).

chested: An arrow shaft that tapers towards the point.

closed stance: When aiming the bow, standing so that archer is turned slightly away from the target.

clout shooting: Shooting at targets using a high trajectory rather than the normal low trajectory.

cock feather: The feather in the fletching that points away from the bow, usually of a different color to aid in quick identification (also called an *index feather*).

composite bow: A bow made from more than one material.

compound bow: A bow that uses cams and multiple strings to "compound" the mechanical advantage of the bowstring.

Crécy, Battle of (1346): Major archery battle in which English bowmen shot over half a million arrows at French troops, killing 10,000 while only losing a few hundred archers themselves.

crest: Colorful stripes along the shaft, used to identify an arrow's owner.

deflex: A designed curve in a bow towards the belly (not to be confused with *follow*, which is a byproduct of strain in the bow).

dominant eye: The eye an archer uses when optics or perspective forces a choice between the two.

draw: The act of pulling the bowstring.

REFERENCE

draw length: The distance from the belly of the bow to the bowstring at full draw.

draw weight: The tension required to pull the bowstring back to full draw.

eccentric pulley: A pulley with an off-center axle; part of a compound bow.

end: One round of shooting a certain number of arrows. After shooting an end, archers retrieve their arrows.

F.I.T.A.: Fédération Internationale de Tir à l'Arc, the international archery governing body that sets competition standards.

face: A flat paper or cloth sheet that covers a target butt, marked with scoring rings or a target design.

fast: An ancient command to stop shooting, such as when someone steps in front of a target. It is thought to be a shortening of "hold fast."

feathers: A natural material that makes superior fletchings.

ferrule cement: A heat-set adhesive used to secure arrowheads to the shaft.

fiberglass: A common man-made bow making material.

field archery: Shooting at either butts or 3D targets, while walking a predetermined course of varying ranges and difficulties.

field point: A type of arrowhead that is heavy, round, and pointed. It is shot into butts, yet is durable enough for stump shooting.

fingers: A three-fingered glove that protects the fingers of the archer from the string.

fistmele: The distance from the belly of the bow to the string at the widest point (pronounced "fist-meelee"). Also known as *brace height*.

flatbow: A bow with wide, flat limbs and no recurve. Usually a self bow.

Fletch-Tite™: A name brand of fletching cement.

Fletch: Nickname of the author; also, a funny Chevy Chase movie that has nothing to do with archery.

fletcher: A person who makes arrows, not to be confused with an *arrowsmith*.

fletching: The rearward part of the arrow that keeps it from tumbling in flight. Though often comprised of three feathers, there are many other configurations available.

fletching cement: An adhesive used for gluing the fletchings onto the shaft.

fletching jig: A special clamp that holds the fletchings on the arrow at the correct angle and position until dry.

fletching tape: A thin double-sided tape that replaces fletching cement.

flight archery: Shooting purely for distance or time aloft.

flu-flu arrow: An arrow with oversized or spiral fletchings, designed to be shot at overhead targets and decelerate quickly if it misses.

follow: An undesirable characteristic of a bow where it retains some of its bend after unstringing (also called *string follow*).

follow through: Maintaining a stable position after the release, to prevent jerking.

foot bow: A large bow designed to be shot while seated, pulling the string with both hands and holding the bow with the feet.

footed arrow: A wooden arrow that has a portion of the shaft near the point made from a different, harder wood.

G.N.A.S.: Grand National Archery Society, a British archery group.

graphite: A strong, light, modern material sometimes used to make arrow shafts.

handle: The part of the bow that the archer grips.

head: See *arrowhead*.

helix: A three-dimensional spiral. Feathers that twist slightly around the shaft are said to be "helically fletched".

hen feathers: The two other feathers of the fletching besides the *cock feather*.

hondo knot: A loop-shaped knot sometimes used at the ends of a bowstring; it is also used in making a lariat.

index feather: The feather in the fletching that points away from the bow, usually of a different color to aid in quick identification (also called a *cock feather*).

instinctive shooting: Aiming without the use of any sighting system.

kaburaya: A whistling Japanese arrowhead.

karimata: A V-shaped Japanese arrowhead, literally, "hunting fork".

kick target: A target intended to be kicked or thrown into a field, then shot at.

kisser button: A bead woven into the bowstring, that rests against the archer's lip at full draw to aid in a consistent anchor point.

kyudo: The Japanese art of archery.

laminated bow: A bow made from multiple thin sheets (laminations) of material.

letoff: On compound bows, the difference between the reduced draw weight at full draw and the maximum draw weight.

longbow: A straight bow that is about as tall as the archer.

loose: A medieval term; to release the arrow.

Mediterranean release: Another name for the standard three-finger release.

Mongolian release: An eastern release style that uses the thumb to hold the bowstring.

nock (n): On an arrow, a cut in the rear to accept the bowstring. On a bow, the grooves towards the tips that hold the bowstring.

nock (v): To place the nock of the arrow onto the bowstring.

nocking point: A string or metal clip that marks the point of the bowstring where the arrow should be consistently nocked.

nocking pliers: A special tool for installing metal *nocking point indicators.*

open stance: When aiming the bow, standing so that archer is turned slightly towards the target.

overbowed: An archer shooting a bow that is too heavy, often causing bad habits and fatigue.

papingo: another name for the *popinjay,* see below.

peep sight: A ring woven into the bowstring above the serving, for the archer to look through as part of a mechanical sight.

pile: An alternate spelling of *pyle.*

pin sight: A mechanical sight comprised of adjustable pins that can be set for differing ranges.

point: An arrowhead that is conical or pointed.

point-of-aim: A barebow sighting system where the archer aims by using the position of the arrowhead relative to a mark on the ground.

point blank range: The range at which the arrow goes neither higher nor lower than where the arrowhead was pointed.

Poitiers, Battle of (1356): A virtual repeat of the Battle of Crécy ten years before, where sound tactics and good archers ruled the day.

popinjay: An artificial bird used as a target in the archery shoot of the same name. See the section on Activities for a lengthier description.

precision: The closeness of an archer's shots to one another. Not to be confused with *accuracy.*

pyle: A historical term for *point.*

quiver: A container for holding arrows.

range: 1) A designated place where archery occurs. 2) The distance from the archer to the target.

recurve: A curve at the tip of a bow's limbs, towards its back (or direction of the target). Also, slang for *recurve bow.*

recurve bow: A bow with recurved limbs.

reflex: Overall curve in a bow towards its back (or direction of the target) when unstrung.

release (n): A mechanical device to aid in releasing the string.

release (v): The act of letting go of the string.

rest: A tiny arm that the arrow rests upon during the draw. Also known as a

Archery Terms

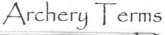

"flipper rest".

riser: Thickened part of the bow above the handle.

Robin Hood: A mythical folk hero and archer from medieval England. Also, a colloquialism for splitting one arrow with another.

rood: An ancient length of measurement. In archery, it's 7 ½ yards. Traditional target distances were in rood increments, such as 12 roods (90 yards), 16 roods (120 yards), etc.

roving mark: A traditional English archery shoot at long, unmarked distances. See the section on Activities for a lengthier description.

score: (1) The point total for an archer when competing. (2) An ancient quantity, meaning twenty. As in, "a score of arrows", or "two score yards."

serving: Extra string wrapped around the bowstring to reinforce areas of excessive wear such as the loops or nocking area.

self bow: A bow made of only one piece of wood (as opposed to a *composite bow*).

shaft: The long, thin portion that makes up the main body of the arrow.

shaftment: An archaic term for the rear portion of the arrow with the fletchings and nock.

sheaf: An ancient quantity, meaning 24 (or two dozen). Arrows sometimes come by the sheaf.

shelf: A flat spot on top of the handle, upon which the arrow rests before shooting.

shoot-through riser: On modern bows, a riser that is cut in towards the centerline of the bow so that the arrow travels on the centerline of the string's motion when shot, reducing archer's paradox.

sight: A device that aids the archer in aiming.

silencer: Bits of fuzz or fur attached to the bowstring to reduce twang or string noise when shooting.

sinew: Animal tendons, sometimes used as a backing on composite bows.

sinistral: Left-handed.

slap: When the bowstring strikes the inside forearm of the archer.

spine weight: A measure of stiffness of the arrow. An arrow with a spine weight matching the draw weight of the bow will bend the correct amount to negate archer's paradox.

stabilizer: A counterweight attached to the bow to reduce minor shakes and trembles.

stack: When a poorly built bow gains weight rapidly at the end of the draw, it is said to "stack". It is both uncomfortable and inefficient.

stance: The way an archer stands while shooting.

"standard arrow": A relatively new convention for shooting historical longbow arrows, this enormous missile is 3/8" diameter, 32" long, and must weigh at least 800 grains.

stave: A piece of wood to be made into a bow, or, a straight bow when unstrung.

straight bow: A bow without recurve, reflex, or deflex.

stele: An old word for the shaft of the arrow.

string (n): See *bowstring*.

string (v): The process of fitting the bowstring onto the bow under tension, making it ready to shoot.

stump shooting: Shooting at random inanimate objects (such as stumps) while walking a spontaneous, unplanned course.

tab: A flat piece of leather or plastic that goes between the archer's fingers and the bowstring, to prevent blisters.

tackle: A generic term that refers to the archer's equipment.

take-down bow: A bow that can be disassembled or folded, to aid in transport or storage.

target: Anything you are shooting at. Not to be confused with *face*.

target archery: Shooting at faces mounted on butts, at predetermined distances on a closed range.

target point: A type of arrowhead that is round with a dull point, and usually made from thin stamped metal. For shooting into target butts only, they are typical on most institutional grade arrows.

teardrop: On a compound bow, a teardrop-shaped metal hook at the end of the cable, to which the bowstring is attached.

thumb ring: A ring worn on the thumb to aid with release when using a Turkish-style draw.

tiller (n): The shape of a bow's curvature when drawn.

tiller (v): In bowmaking, to scrape away wood until the bow curves correctly when bent.

toxophilite: A lover of archery.

vanes: Fletchings made from plastic, vinyl, or leather.

wand: A thin vertical piece of wood used as a target.

wood: A great thing to make bows and arrows out of.

yabusame: A Japanese ceremony where an archer shoots at targets while riding a galloping horse.

Further Reading

Archery, like much of life, is treated differently by different cultures and individuals. The styles and techniques vary widely, and many times one person's opinion will be the exact opposite of another's. Good and prudent archery instructors should learn as much as possible from many different sources, and use their own personal experience and experimentation to devise an archery program that is the best for their students.

Older books are excellent sources for information on shooting style, technique, and history, but can be a bit outdated when it comes to current equipment, materials, and regulations. If possible, read both old and new books. Here follows a list of books that might be useful to archery instructors, either as technical resources, inspiration, or entertainment.

TECHNICAL & INSTRUCTIONAL

Know the Sport: Archery, by John Adams (1994). A thin, fast overview of the general things you need to know to get an arrow moving towards a target. It contains large, clear photographs. Archery programs with relatively inexperienced instructors should have a copy of this available.

Archery (Boy Scouts of America merit badge series), Boy Scouts of America (current edition). Scouting has incorporated archery into its program since the beginning, and many youngsters got their first experience with it through Scouting, myself included. Even if you are not involved with Scouting, they produce a useful body of archery knowledge worth exploring.

Bow & Arrow, by Larry Wise (1992). A more technical look at various aspects of archery, such as bow tuning and equipment selection.

Beginners Guide to Traditional Archery, by Brian J. Sorrells (2004). Although mostly intended for bowhunters, this book has a good practice regime for barebow shooters. It also has good information on bare-bow tuning.

EQUIPMENT MAKING AND REPAIR

The Traditional Bowyer's Bible, vols. 1-3, ed. by Jim Hamm (1992). This three-book series is <u>the</u> definitive word on modern traditional archery. It is more advanced than would be needed for beginning institutional archery instruction, but if you want to truly understand how recurves and longbows work, this is the book. It also includes sections on making bowstrings, arrows, quivers, and more.

How to Make Recurve Bows and Matched Arrows, by Patrick E. Spielman (1964). This book is somewhat dated, but has good do-it-yourself examples of how to make bows and arrows from scratch, using basic shop tools.

Archery Tackle: How to Make and How to Use It, by Adolph Shane (1936). Another dated but useful book on how to make bows and arrows, with a good section specifically on arrows.

INSPIRATION & ENTERTAINMENT

The White Archer, by James Houston (1967). An Inuit legend, this book is a moving tale about a young archer surviving in the frozen north. The illustrated story is inspiring and would be an excellent tale to read to young archers.

Zen in the Art of Archery, by Eugen Herrigel (1953). This book is mostly philosophical, rather than a technical description of archery, but would be interesting to someone who wanted to more fully explore the spiritual and emotional aspects of archery.

HISTORICAL & BIOGRAPHICAL

Though many books have been written on archery, there are three that are generally considered the most important in spawning the resurgence of modern archery. They are *The Witchery of Archery* (1879), *Hunting with the Bow and Arrow* (1923), and *Hunting the Hard Way* (1953). A serious student of archery should get around to reading all three; none are very long, and they capture the emotion and spirit of archery, as well as providing technical information on shooting and equipment.

Toxophilus, by Roger Ascham (1545). This was the first archery book ever written in English. Much like Shakespeare and Chaucer, the archaic language and erratic spelling are trying at times. Nevertheless, it's fascinating and gives a good perspective on the finer points of archery, many of which haven't changed in 500 years. The edited & commented version by Peter Medine (2002) is helpful and provides explanation to Ascham's occasional cryptic passages.

The Witchery of Archery, by Maurice Thompson (1878). Once you become accustomed to the Victorian writing style, this is a pleasant little book extolling the virtues of archery and recounting tales of archery adventure. It was the driving force behind archery's resurgence in America in the late 1800s.

Hunting With the Bow and Arrow, by Saxton Pope (1923). Though much of this book is stories of bowhunting, it has several chapters on making traditional equipment. Of particular interest are the first four chapters, which describe the archery of Ishi, the last wild Native American.

Hunting the Hard Way, by Howard Hill (1953). This easy-reading book is an account of the amazing exploits of the world's greatest archer, by the man himself. Though much of it focuses on hunting rather than archery instruction, it has several chapters on equipment making and selection, as well as many amusing archery anecdotes.

Ishi in Two Worlds: A Biography of the Last Wild Indian in North America, by Theodora Kroeber (1961). Though only a small portion of this book deals with Native American archery technique, it is a worthwhile, moving account of the life and death of a man and a culture.

The Crooked Stick, by Hugh D.H. Soar (2005). Mr. Soar is a celebrated archery historian with an extensive list of honors, and this book is his summary of how the longbow evolved from prehistory to modern day. It is well-researched and scholarly, yet remains readable and interesting to even the casual archer.

EQUIPMENT & MATERIALS

3Rivers Archery
www.threeriversarchery.com

They boast that they are the "world's largest traditional archery supplier". Although I am unable to verify that, I **do** know that they have just about everything you could imagine for traditional archery. It's also a small, family-owned business with great customer service; I highly recommend them.

Ace Archery Tackle
www.bowsite2.com/aceshopping/index.asp

Broadheads, field points, and other arrow heads. Some miscellaneous archery paraphernalia like spine testers. Interestingly, Ace was one of the first companies to mass produce broadheads, back in 1927.

Trueflight Manufacturing Co.
www.trueflightfeathers.com

Feather fletching materials of all shapes, sizes, and colors. The website also has information on selecting & installing feather fletchings.

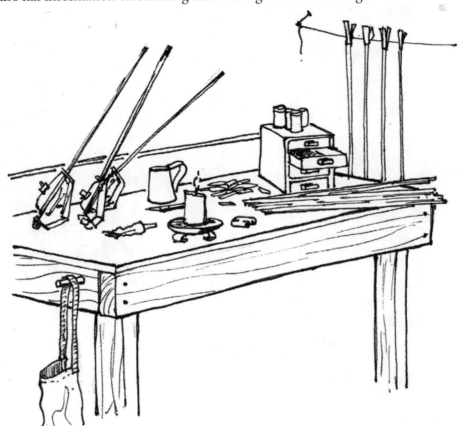

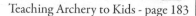

ARCHERY ORGANIZATIONS

There are numerous archery organizations, both national and international, so I won't try to list them all. Many serve a specific niche of archery, but they all can be helpful places to turn for more information about this ancient art.

FITA- Fédération International de Tir à l'Arc
www.archery.org

This is the international archery organization that sets standards for competition, makes rules, and administers the archery events in the Olympics.

The Fraternity of St. George

Originally founded in 1509, it has been reborn to continue the tradition of heavy English longbow shooting. It's based in the UK.

GNAS- Grand National Archery Society
www.gnas.org

GNAS is the governing body for archery in Great Britain, and administers rules for some events that aren't part of normal international competition, as well as rounds that are shot in Imperial units.

National Archery Association
www.usarchery.org

This is the original American archery society founded by the Thompson brothers in 1879. It has since evolved into the body responsible for Olympic archery training in the US, as well as offering training and certification for archery instructors and coaches.

International Bowhunting Organization
www.ibo.net

Although bowhunting is beyond the scope of this book, this organization has resources available for tournaments, training, and equipment. It would be a good jumping-off point to learn more about bowhunting, as well.

National Field Archery Association
www.fieldarchery.org

Founded in 1939, this American group exists to promote field archery.

ARCHERY WEBSITES

The internet has changed the way people learn and gather information about the world around them, and archers are no exception. I am hesitant to list a lot of archery websites, as they tend to come and go without notice. Also, since they aren't as carefully edited as print media, some contain misinformation or are too poorly organized to be of much use. But there are a few good ones, so I will present them here— in the hopes that they will still be as good by the time you get around to visiting them!

www.stickbow.com: If you took a heap of information about traditional archery and put it all in one place, you'd have Stickbow.com. There are articles about history, arrow construction, bow construction, shooting technique, and hunting tricks. They also have an extensive list of suppliers and advertisers that sell all sorts of archery equipment, supplies, tools, and raw materials.

www.longbow-archers.com: This site is dedicated solely to longbow shooting, but it's got a wealth of interesting information about the history of the longbow, its rebirth in the modern age, and descriptions of some of the weirder historical shoots. If you are in Europe, it is also handy for its list of European shooting clubs and societies.

www.archerylibrary.com: Generally, copyrights expire 70 years after the death of the author. This site, maintained by Terry Trier, catalogs and makes available many great archery works that are now in the public domain.

www.bowsite.com: Besides being a clever pun, this site also has a mountain of links to archery equipment suppliers and businesses that cater to archery. It is heavily slanted towards the bowhunting crowd.

And finally, don't forget **www.teachingarchery.com**, a site dedicated to teaching kids about archery. You can download target faces, teaching aids, patterns for equipment, find links to archery suppliers and organizations, and buy more copies of this book for your friends and coworkers!

Now more than ever, this knowledge needs to be available so the ancient and noble art of Archery will stay alive in days to come. During my years of teaching archery at summer camps, I noticed that many archery instructors were woefully under-equipped in terms of both equipment and training. No book like this existed at the time, so I hope that this book finds a useful home in the hands and hearts of archery instructors everywhere.

DEDICATION

Writing this book was a labor of love, and I would like to dedicate it to:

➺ My grandfather, for discovering archery during its Golden Age of rebirth, and passing the ancient art on to his son.

➺ My father, not only for showing me the ways of the bow, but for showing me the importance of the woods and water. I will forever be your son.

➺ My brother, for going shooting with me when no one else would.

➺ Anyone who donates their time and heart to work at summer camp.

➺ All the kids that taught me how important it is to pass this knowledge along.

THANKS

I have found the following people invaluable in the process of producing this book, and can't thank them enough for their time, knowledge, and enthusiasm:

➺ Mark Schneider: blacksmith, friend, and archery companion.

➺ Frank Victoria: friend, cover illustrator, and author of the *Kilt le Picte* series of children's books.

➺ Missy Schneider: for proofreading, and reminding me how important camp is.

➺ Mom: for getting me my first archery job before I could even drive.

➺ Andy Johnson: bowyer, who helped me make my first bow.

And, of course, my wife and fellow camp counselor Ruby deserves a lot of credit for always encouraging my scattered, crazy pursuits.

FLETCH.

REFERENCE

ABOUT THE AUTHOR

Jim "Fletch" Fanjoy has over 25 years of archery experience, and has instructed hundreds of young archers at summer camps across the country. He makes his own bows, arrows, and tackle. Archery is a generations-old tradition in his family, being passed down from his grandfather (a champion archer in California in the early fifties) to his father to him.

May the gods grant us all the space to carry a sturdy bow and wander through the forest glades to seek the bounding deer; to lie in deep meadow grasses; to watch the flight of birds; to smell the fragrances of burning leaves; to cast an upward glance at the unobserved beauty of the moon. May they give us the strength to draw the string to the cheek, the arrow to the barb and loose the flying shaft, so long as life may last.

~Saxton Pope

Made in the USA